Y0-BGG-831

GERMAN
In Your Pocket

NEW
HOLLAND

GLOBETROTTER™

Second edition published in 2012
by New Holland Publishers Ltd
London • Cape Town • Sydney
• Auckland
10 9 8 7 6 5 4 3 2 1

website:
www.newhollandpublishers.com

Garfield House, 86 Edgware Road
London W2 2EA
United Kingdom

Wembley Square, First Floor
Solan Road
Cape Town 8001
South Africa

Unit 1, Gibbes Street
Chatswood, NSW 2067
Australia

218 Lake Road
Northcote, Auckland
New Zealand

Publishing Manager:
Thea Grobbelaar
Designer: Lellyn Creamer
Cover Design: Nicole Bannister
Illustrator: Marisa Roman
Editor: Thea Grobbelaar
Translator: Friedel Herrmann
Proofreader: Claudia dos Santos

Reproduction by Resolution, Cape Town
Printed and bound by Times Offset (M)
Sdn. Bhd., Malaysia

Copyright © 2012 in text:
Friedel Herrmann
Copyright © 2012 in photograph:
Rex Butcher/Jon Arnold Images
Copyright © 2012 in illustrations:
Marisa Galloway
Copyright © 2012 New Holland
Publishers (UK) Ltd

ISBN 978 1 78009 399 4

Cover photograph: *Dinkelsbuhl,
Bavaria, Germany.*

CONTENTS

PHRASE BOOK

DICTIONARY

This PHRASE BOOK is thematically colour-coded for easy use and is organized according to the situation you're most likely to be in when you need it. The fairly comprehensive DICTIONARY section consists of two parts – English/German and German/English.

To make speaking German easy, we encourage our readers to memorize some general PRONUNCIATION rules (*see* page 8). After you have familiarized yourself with the basic tools of the language and the rudiments of German GRAMMAR (*see* page 14), all you need to do is turn to the appropriate section of the phrase book and find the words you need to make yourself understood. If the selection is not exactly what you're looking for, consult the dictionary for other options.

Just to get you started, here are some German expressions you might have heard, read or used at some time: *Schadenfreude*, *Wunderkind*, *Götterdämmerung*, *Leitmotiv*, *Gemütlichkeit*. Even if you are unfamiliar with these words and would rather not try to say them out loud, just remain confident, follow our easy advice and practise a little, and you will soon master useful phrases for everyday life. Speak slowly and enunciate carefully and your counterpart is likely to follow suit.

Some German words, especially those ending in -ion, are pronounced differently from their English equivalents (e.g. Situation – *zee too ah tsiohn*), or else changed just slightly (modernization – *Modernisierung*), though their meanings remain clear. Nowadays many English terms are used in German, especially in business, sport and leisure activities, so everyone will know what you mean when you say things like 'laptop', 'golf' and 'tennis'.

A section on HOLIDAYS AND FESTIVALS (*see* page 82) provides some background knowledge so that you know what you're celebrating and why. There's no better way to learn a language than joining in some enjoyment!

The brief section on manners, mannerisms and ETIQUETTE (*see* page 76) can help you make sense of the people around you. Make an effort to view your host country and its people tolerantly – that way you will be open to the new experience and able to enjoy it.

Learning a new language can be a wonderful but frightening experience. It is not the object of this book to teach you perfect German, but rather to equip you with just enough knowledge for a successful holiday or business trip. Luckily you are unlikely to be criticized on your grammatical correctness when merely asking for directions. The most important thing is to make yourself understood. To this end a brief section on grammar and a guide to pronunciation have been included in this book. There is, however, no substitute for listening to native speakers.

Before you leave, it might be a good idea to familiarize yourself with the sections on Pronunciation, Grammar and Etiquette. This can easily be done en route to your destination. You will also benefit from memorizing a few important phrases before you go.

The sections of the Phrase Book are arranged by topic for quick reference. Simply go to the contents list (*see* page 3) to find the topic you need. The Dictionary section (*see* page 88) goes both ways, helping you to understand and be understood.

Abbreviations have been used in those instances where one English word could be interpreted as more than one part of speech, e.g. 'smoke' (a noun, the substance coming from a fire) and 'smoke' (a verb, what one would do with a cigarette). Here is a list of these and some other abbreviations used in this book:

vb	verb
n	noun
adj	adjective
adv	adverb
pol	polite
fam	familiar (informal)
elec	electric/al
med	medical
anat	anatomy
rel	religion

The gender and number of German nouns have been specified as follows:

m	masculine
f	feminine
n	neutral
pl	plural

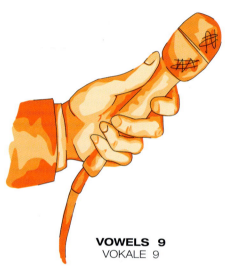

German is a phonetic language, so a bit of practice imprints the sounds, and you can soon read most of it. Many letters are pronounced much like the English equivalent.

   Some letters have no equivalent in English: ß has been substituted with ss where possible, to make it easier to read.

VOWELS
VOKALE

Here are some vowels in German:

- ◆ **a** (long) – like the **a** in far – *sagen*
- ◆ **a** (short) – like the **u** in cut – *Katze*
- ◆ **e** (long) – like the first **e** in where – *legen*
- ◆ **e** (short) – like the **e** in bet – *Leck*
- ◆ **i** (long) – like the **i** in sing – *singen*
- ◆ **i** (short) – like the **i** in bit – *Witz*
- ◆ **o** – like the **o** in sock – *trocken*
- ◆ **u** – like the **oo** in foot – *lustig*

Using the Umlaut on a vowel changes its sound:

- ◆ **ä** – like the **a** in care – *käse*
- ◆ **ö** – like the **er** in loser – *böse*
- ◆ **ü** – similar to the **ur** in spur; also similar to the **ee** in feel, <u>but</u> pronounced with the lips forming an **o** – *süss*

Diphthongs are pronounced as follows:

- au – like the **ow** in h**ow** – *blau*
- eu – like the **oy** in b**oy** – *heute*
- äu – like the **oy** in b**oy** – *Mäuse*
- ei – like the **i** in size – *keine*
- ie – like the **ea** in **ea**sy – *diese*

NB An **e** at the end of a word is always pronounced – *bitte* sounds like bitter.

CONSONANTS
KONSONANTEN

- **sch** – pronounced **sh** – *Schule*
- **ch** – has no equivalent in English (except in the Scottish word 'lo**ch**'), and is a guttural sound that needs practice.
- **ch** – at the beginning of a word, this is usually pronounced like **k** in English. In German it is usually a foreign word, e.g. *Chrysanthemen, Chirurg, Chronik*. It is also sometimes pronounced with a hissing sound, e.g. *China*.
- **ch** – in the middle of a word, it is either a guttural sound (as in *lachen, machen*) or a hissing sound (as in *Licht, nicht*); on pages 12 and 13 the hissing sound is indicated by *kh.*

THE LETTER S
DER BUCHSTABE S

- ◆ **S** – at the beginning of a word, it is pronounced **z** – *Sonne*
- ◆ **s** – after a vowel, it is pronounced **z** – *Hose*
- ◆ **s** – at the end of a word, it is pronounced **s** – *Gras*
- ◆ **s** – after a consonant, it is pronounced **s** – *Kunst*
- ◆ **s** – when followed by **p** or **t**, it is pronounced **sh** – *springen, still*

OTHER CONSONANTS
ANDERE KONSONANTEN

- ◆ **b** – at the end of a word, it is pronounced **p** – *gib*
- ◆ **d** – at the end of a word, it is pronounced **t** – *und*
- ◆ **g** – at the end of a word, it is pronounced somewhere between a **g** and a **k** – *Tag*
- ◆ **v** – is pronounced **f** (*Vater*), with a few exceptions like *Klavier* and *Vase*, where it is pronounced **v**
- ◆ **w** – is pronounced **v** (*Welle*)

And remember: German is enunciated clearly.

PRONUNCIATION

Practise a few phrases in German (the stressed syllables are underlined:

Guten Tag!
goo-ten tahk
Good day!

Auf Wiedersehen!
owf vee-der-zehn
Goodbye!

Sprechen Sie Englisch?
shpray-khen zee ang-lish
Do you speak English?

Bitte langsam sprechen!
bit-ter lahng-sahm shpray-khen
Please speak slowly!

Ich verstehe nicht!
ikh fer-shtayer nikht
I don't understand

Wie geht es Ihnen?
vee-gayt-ess-ee-nen
How are you? (polite)

Wie geht es Dir?
vee-gayt-ess-deer
How are you? (familiar)

Danke, gut!
dang-keh goot
Fine, thanks!

Ich möchte ...
ikh muekhter (ue is pronounced like the u in fur)
I'd like ...

Bitte? Wie bitte?
bit-ter – vee bit-ter
Pardon?

Bitte!

bit-ter

Please! (also means: You're welcome!)

Danke!

dang-keh

Thank you!

Verzeihung!

fer-tsy-oong

Sorry! Pardon!

Wo sind die Toiletten?

voh zint dee twah-let-ten

Where are the toilets?

Darf ich …?

dahf ikh

May I …?

Gestern

gays-stern

yesterday

Heute

hoy-ter

today

Morgen

mohr-gan

tomorrow

Darf ich telefonieren?

dahf ikh telephoneeren?

May I use the phone?

Wo ist das?

voh ist dus?

Where is it?

Wo (Wann) können wir uns treffen?

voh (vunn) kuennen veer oonz traifen (ue is pronounced like the u in fur)

Where (When) can we meet?

The grammar section has deliberately been kept very brief as this is not a language course.

A note on the Umlaut:
Sometimes, if you are using technology that has become outdated, accents such as the Umlaut are not available. There is a way to indicate that an Umlaut should be used – just add the letter **e** after the letter which needs the accent. Elektrizität (electricity), for example, can be written as Elektrizitaet, or Kühlschrank (fridge) as Kuehlschrank.

NOUNS
NOMEN
All German nouns begin with a **capital letter**.

There are three **genders** (masculine, feminine and neuter) reflected in the **article**:
- *der/ein Mann* – the/a man
- *die/eine Frau* – the/a woman
- *das/ein Kind* – the/a child

The **plural article** (in the Nominative case, see page 16) is the same for all genders: *die*

Some nouns can have more than one gender, and they change their meaning according to their gender. For example, the noun *Band*, if it is masculine, means 'book' or 'volume', whereas its feminine form means 'band' (music) and its neuter form means 'ribbon'; *Kiefer*, if masculine, means 'jaw', but in its feminine form it means 'pine tree'.

There are four **cases**:

- **Nominative** (subject) – *der/ein, die/eine, das/ein*
- **Accusative** (direct object) – *den/einen, die/eine, das/ein*
- **Genitive** (possessive) – *dessen/eines, deren/einer, dessen/eines*
- **Dative** (indirect object) – *dem/einem, der/einer, dem/einem*

NB Since the article varies, depending on the inflection (case), the gender of the nouns in the dictionary section is only stated as **m** (masculine), **f** (feminine) or **n** (neuter). A sustained effort is required to memorize all the genders and declensions, but this is not vital in order to make yourself understood.

PRONOUNS
PRONOMEN

In the nominative case, pronouns are easy to learn: **I** (*ich*), **you** (*du*), **he** (*er*), **she** (*sie*), **it** (*es*), **we** (*wir*), **you plural** (*ihr*), **they** (*sie*). The polite form of 'you' is *Sie*, written with a capital letter.

In the other cases pronouns can be a bit more tricky, but having them all together in tabular form will help you to make more sense of them. The abbreviations 'fam' and 'pol' have been used here to distinguish between the familiar and polite forms, and 'pl' indicates the plural of 'you':

Direct Object		Indirect Object	
me	mich	(to) me	mir
you	dich (fam)	(to) you	dir (fam)
you	Sie (pol)	(to) you	Ihnen (pol)
him	ihn	(to) him	ihm
her	sie	(to) her	ihr
it	es	(to) it	ihm
us	uns	(to) us	uns
you	euch (pl)	(to) you	euch (pl)
them	sie	(to) them	ihnen

Reflexive Pronoun		Possessive Pronoun	
myself	mich	mine	mein/e
yourself	dich (fam)	yours	dein/e (fam)
yourself	sich (pol)	yours	Ihr/e (pol)
himself	sich	his	sein/e
herself	sich	hers	ihr/e
itself	sich	its	sein/e
ourselves	uns	ours	unser/e
yourselves	euch	yours	euer/e (pl)
themselves	sich	theirs	ihr/e

Wer can be used as an indefinite pronoun with the meaning of 'whoever':

◆ **Wer zuletzt lacht, lacht am besten** – Whoever laughs last, laughs longest.

◆ **Wer nicht hören will, muss fühlen** – Whoever won't hear, must feel.

VERBS

VERBEN

AUXILIARY VERBS (HILFSVERBEN)

It would be a good idea to familiarize yourself with the present and past tense of the main auxiliary verbs (to have and to be):

SEIN – to be

PRESENT TENSE
ich bin – I am
du bist – you are
er/sie ist – he/she is
wir sind – we are
ihr seid – you (pl) are
sie sind – they are

PAST TENSE
ich war – I was
du warst – you were
er/sie war – he/she was
wir waren – we were
ihr wart – you (pl) were
sie waren – they were

HABEN – to have

PRESENT TENSE
ich habe – I have
du hast – you have
er/sie hat – he/she has
wir haben – we have
ihr habt – you (pl) have
sie haben – they have

PAST TENSE
ich hatte – I had
du hattest – you had
er/sie hatte – he/she had
wir hatten – we had
ihr hattet – you (pl) had
sie hatten – they had

NEGATIVE FORM (VERNEINUNG)
To make a participle negative, add nicht:
- *Ich habe geschlafen* – I slept
- *Ich habe nicht geschlafen* – I didn't sleep

But **ein/eine/einen** becomes **kein/keine/keinen**:

◆ *Ich habe ein Glas* – I have a glass
◆ *Ich habe kein Glas* – I have no glass

ADJECTIVES OF NATIONALITY
NATIONALITÄTSANZEIGENDE ADJEKTIVE

NOUN	ADJECTIVE
der Engländer, die Engländerin	englisch
der Franzose, die Französin	französisch
der Deutsche, die Deutsche	deutsch

Note that adjectives of nationality are written with a small letter, because they are indeed adjectives – only nouns are written with a capital letter in German. However, when adjectives are formed from the names of towns and countries by adding **-er**, these are written with a capital letter (because they are considered to be part of a name), for example *Berliner Kinder* and *Schweizer Käse*.

WORD ORDER
WORTSTELLUNG

- ◆ Participles and infinitives normally come at the end of the clause: *Ich habe die Frau im Garten gesehen.*
- ◆ In a subordinate clause the auxiliary comes last of all: *Der Patient, den wir gestern besucht haben, war sehr krank.*
- ◆ Adverbs usually come in the following order – time, manner, place: *Ich fahre jeden Morgen mit der U-Bahn zur Arbeit.*
- ◆ Reflexive pronouns come early in the clause: *Ich habe mich verletzt.*

FORMING FRACTIONS
MATHEMATISCHER BRÜCHE BILDEN

Fractions are formed as follows:

- ◆ -**tel** is added to the cardinal number from 4-19: *drei Fünftel*
- ◆ -**stel** is added from 20 onwards: *drei Zwanzigstel*
- ◆ half – *die Hälfte* (noun), *halb* (adjective)
- ◆ a third – *ein Drittel*

For more numbers, see page 23.

NUMBERS
ZAHLEN

0	null *(nool)*
1	eins *(ines)*
2	zwei *(tsvy)*
3	drei *(dry)*
4	vier *(feer)*
5	fünf *(foonf)*
6	sechs *(zex)*
7	sieben *(zee-ben)*
8	acht *(akht)*
9	neun *(noyne)*
10	zehn *(tsain)*
11	elf *(elf)*
12	zwölf *(tsvoolf)*
13	dreizehn *(dry-tsain)*
14	vierzehn *(feer-tsain)*
15	fünfzehn *(foonf-tsain)*
16	sechzehn *(sekh-tsain)*
17	siebzehn *(zeep-tsain)*
18	achtzehn *(akht-tsain)*
19	neunzehn *(noyne-tsen)*
20	zwanzig *(tsvan-tsik)*
21	ein-und-zwanzig *(ine-oond-tsvan-tsik)*
22	zwei-und-zwanzig *(tsvy-oond-tsvan-tsik)*
30	dreissig *(dry-sick)*

40	vierzig *(fear-tsik)*
50	fünfzig *(foonf-tsik)*
60	sechzig *(sekh-tsik)*
70	siebzig *(zeep-tsik)*
80	achtzig *(akht-tsik)*
90	neunzig *(noyne-tsik)*
100	hundert *(hoon-dirt)*
101	hundert-eins *(hoon-dert-ines)*
120	hundert-zwanzig *(hoon-dert-tsvan-sick)*
200	zweihundert *(tsvy-hoondert)*
1000	tausend *(tow-sent)*
1 million	eine Million *(ine mill-yohn)*
1 billion	eine Milliarde *(ine mill-yarde)*
1st	erste/r/s *(airs-te)*
2nd	zweite/r/s *(tsvy-te)*
3rd	dritte/r/s *(dree-te)*
4th	vierte/r/s *(feer-te)*
5th	fünfte/r/s *(foonf-te)*
6th	sechste/r/s *(zex-te)*
7th	siebte/r/s *(zeep-te)*
8th	achte/r/s *(akh-te)*
9th	neunte/r/s *(noyn-te)*
10th	zehnte/r/s *(tsain-te)*

DAYS TAGE	**MONTHS** MONATE
Monday Montag (_morn_-targ)	**January** Januar (_yaa_-noo-are)
Tuesday Dienstag (_deens_-targ)	**February** Februar (_fay_-brew-are)
Wednesday Mittwoch (_mit_-vokh)	**March** März (Maerz) (_merrts_)
Thursday Donnerstag (_don_-ners-targ)	**April** April (up-_rill_)
Friday Freitag (_fry_-targ)	**May** Mai (_my_)
Saturday Samstag/Sonnabend (_zums_-targ/ _zonn_-are-bent)	**June** Juni (_yoo_-nee)
Sunday Sonntag (_zonn_-targ)	**July** Juli (_yoo_-lee)
weekday Wochentag (_vo_-khen-targ)	**August** August (ow-_goost_)
weekend Wochenende (_vo_-khen-_ain_-de)	**September** September (sep-_tem_-bur)
public holidays öffentliche Feiertage (_oof_-fent-li-khe _fy_-er-tar-ge)	**October** Oktober (oc-_tore_-bur)
	November November (noh-_vem_-ber)

December
Dezember (de-_tsem_-ber)

TIME
ZEIT

---

in the morning
morgens/vormittags
(_mor_-gents/_fore_-mit-tugs)

in the afternoon
am Nachmittag
(um _nakh_-mit-tug)

in the evening
abends/am Abend
(_are_-bents/um _ar_-bent)

What is the time?
Wie spät ist es? Wieviel
Uhr ist es?
(_vee shpate_ ist ess/
vee-feel _oor_ ist ess)

♦ **it's three o'clock**
♦ es ist drei Uhr
   (ess ist _dry_ oor

♦ **it's half past two**
♦ es ist halb drei
   (ess ist _hulp_ dry)

♦ **it's quarter to three**
♦ es ist viertel vor drei
   (ess ist _feer_-till for dry)

♦ **it's twenty past two**
♦ es ist twanzig nach zwei
   (ess ist _tswan_-tsikg
   nakh _tsvy_)

♦ **early**
♦ früh (froo)

♦ **late**
♦ spät (shpate)

at 10 a.m. (10:00)
um zehn Uhr
(oom _tsain_ oor)

at 5 p.m. (17:00)
um siebzehn Uhr
(oom _zeep_-tsain oor)

today
heute (_hoy_-ter)

tomorrow
morgen (_more_-gain)

yesterday
gestern (_gays_-tern)

day after tomorrow
übermorgen
(_oo_-ber-_more_-gayn)

day before yesterday
vorgestern
(_fore_-gays-tern)

this morning
heute Morgen *(hoy-te more-gayn)*

yesterday evening
gestern Abend *(gays-tern ar-bend)*

tomorrow morning
morgen früh *(more-gayn froo)*

last night
gestern Abend *(gays-tern ar-bend)*

this week
diese Woche *(dee-ze wor-khe)*

next week
nächste Woche *(naykh-ste wor-khe)*

now
jetzt *(yets)*

What is today's date?
Der Wievielte ist heute? *(der vee-feel-te ist hoy-te)*

It's 20 December
Heute ist der zwanzigste Dezember *(hoyte ist der tsvan-tseeg-ste de-tsem-bur)*

Good morning
Guten Morgen *(goo-tain more-gain)*

Good afternoon
Guten Tag *(goo-tain targ)*

Good evening
Guten Abend *(goo-tain are-bend)*

Good night
Gute Nacht *(goo-te nakht)*

Hello, Cheerio
Hallo, Tschüss *(harlo, tshewss)*

Goodbye
Auf Wiedersehen *(owf vee-der-zain)*

See you soon
Bis bald *(biss bult)*

See you later
Bis später *(biss shpate-ter)*

Have a good trip
Gute Reise *(goo-te rye-ze)*

Take care
Alles Gute *(ul-less goo-te)*

Have a good time
Viel Vergnügen
(feel fur-gnoo-gen)

I have to go now
Ich muss jetzt gehen
(ikh mooss yets gayne)

It was very nice
Es war sehr schön
(ess var serr shurn)

My name is ...
Ich heisse ... *(ikh hizer ...)*

What is your name?
Wie heisst du? (fam)
(vee hized doo)
Wie ist Ihr name? (pol)
(vee ist eer nar-me)

Pleased to meet you!
Sehr erfreut! Angenehm!
(zer err-froyt, un-ge-name)

How are you?
Wie geht es Ihnen? (pol.)
(vee gait ess ee-nen)
Wie geht es dir? (fam.)
(vee gail ess door)

Just a minute
Einen Augenblick, bitte
(inen ow-gen-blick, bitter)

GENERAL
ALLGEMEIN

Do you speak English?
Sprechen Sie Englisch?
(shpra-khen zee ang-lish)

I don't understand
Ich verstehe nicht
(ikh fer-shtayer nikht)

Please speak very slowly
Bitte ganz langsam sprechen *(bitter gants lung-zum shprai-khen)*

Please repeat that
Bitte sagen Sie das noch einmal *(bitter sar-gen zee dars nokh ine-marl)*

Please write it down
Bitte schreiben Sie es auf
(bitter shrai-ben zee ess owf)

Excuse me please
Entschuldigen Sie bitte
(ant-shool-dee-gen zee bitter)

Could you help me?
Können Sie mir helfen?
(curn-nen zee meer hel-fen)

Could you do me a favour?
Können Sie mir einen Gefallen tun? *(curn-nen zee meer inen gay-fal-len toon)*

Can you show me ...
Können Sie mir zeigen ...? *(curn-nen zee meer tsye-gen ...)*

how?
wie? *(vee)*

where?
wo? *(vore)*

when?
wann? *(vunne)*

who?
wer? *(verr)*

why?
warum? *(va-room)*

which?
welche/r/s? *(vel-khe/r/s)*

I need ...
ich brauche ... *(ikh brwo-khe ...)*

please
bitte *(dun-ke)*

FORMS & SIGNS
FORMULARE UND SCHILDER

Please complete in block letters
Bitte in Druckbuchstaben ausfüllen *(bitter in drook-bookh-shtar-ben ows-fur-len)*

Surname
Nachname *(nakh-nar-me)*

First name
Vorname *(for-nar-me)*

Date of birth
Geburtsdatum *(gay-boorts-dar-toom)*

Place of birth
Geburtsort *(gay-boorts-ort)*

Occupation
Beruf *(bear-roof)*

Nationality
Staatsangehörigkeit *(shtarts-arn-gay-hur-rig-kite)*

Address
Anschrift/Wohnanschrift *(arn-shrift)*

Passport Number
Passnummer
(*pus*-noo-mer)

I.D. Number
Ausweisnummer
(*ows*-vice-noom-mer)

Issued at
Ausgestellt in
(*ows*-gay-shtelt *in*)

Date of arrival
Ankunft, Ankunftsdatum
(*arn*-koonft, *arn*-koonfts-*dar*-toom)

Date of departure
Abreise, Abfahrtsdatum
(*arb*-rizer, *arb*-farts-*dar*-toom)

Engaged, Vacant
Besetzt, Frei
(bay-*zetsed*, fry)

No trespassing
Betreten verboten (bay-*tray*-tern fer-*bore*-ten)

Out of order
Ausser Betrieb (*ows*-sir bay-*troob*)

Please don't disturb
Bitte nicht stören
(bitter nikht *shtur*-ren)

Push, Pull
Drücken, Ziehen (*drew*-ken, *tsee*-hen)

Adults and Children
Erwachsene und Kinder
(air-*vax*-sen-ne oont *kin*-der)

Lift, Elevator
Fahrstuhl, Aufzug
(*far*-stool, *owf*-tsoog)

Escalator
Rolltreppe
(*rawl*-traipe-pe)

Wet paint
Frisch gestrichen
(frish gay-*shtree*-khen)

Open, Closed
Geöffnet / Offen,
Geschlossen / Zu
(gay-*urf*-net / off-fen, gay-*shloss*-sen / tsoo)

Till/Cash Desk
Kasse (cuss-se)

Opening hours
Öffnungszeiten
(urf-noongs-*tsai*-ten)

Self-service
Selbstbedienung
(zelbst-ber-*dee*-noong)

BUS/TRAM STOP
H (HALTESTELLE)

Where is the bus (tram) stop?
Wo ist die Bus- (Strassenbahn-) Haltestelle? *(voh ist dee boos- [shtra-sen-barn] hull-ter-shte-lle)*

Which bus do I take?
Welchen Bus muss ich nehmen? *(val-khen boos mousse ikh nay-men)*

How often do the buses go?
Wie oft fahren die Busse? *(vee oft faa-ren dee boo-sse)*

When is the last bus?
Wann fährt der letzte Bus? *(vann fert der lets-te boos)*

Punch your ticket
Fahrschein entwerten *(far-shine ent-ver-ten)*

I want to go to ...
Ich möchte nach ... *(ikh mur'kh-te nåkh ...)*

Where must I go?
Wo muss ich hingehen? *(voh mousse ikh hin-gain)*

What's the fare to ... ?
Wieviel kostet eine Karte nach ... ? *(vee-feal coss-tet ine car-te nokh)*

Which ticket must I buy?
Welche Karte muss ich kaufen? *(val-khe car-te mousse ikh cow-fen)*

When is the next bus?
Wann geht der nächste Bus? *(vann gait der nex-te boos)*

Do I have to change?
Muss ich umsteigen? *(mousse ikh oom-shtai-gen)*

UNDERGROUND/ SUBWAY/METRO
U (U-BAHN)

entrance, exit
Eingang, Ausgang *(ine-gung, ous-gung)*

Where is the underground station?
Wo ist der U-Bahnhof? *(voh ist der oo-barn-hof)*

inner zone, outer zone
Innenzone, Aussenzone
(*in*-nen-tsoh-ne, *ous*-sen-tsoh-ne)

Do you have a map for the metro?
Haben Sie eine Karte für die U-Bahn Linien? (*har*-ben zee ine *car*-te foor dee *oo*-barn *lee*-nee-en)

I want to go to ...
Ich möchte nach ... (ikh *mur'kh*-te nakh ...)

Can you give me change?
Können Sie wechseln? (*cur*-nen zee *vex*-eln)

Where must I go?
Wo muss ich hingehen? (voh mousse ikh *hin*-gain)

When is the next train?
Wann geht der nächste Zug? (*vann* gait der *nex*-te *tsoog*)

How long will it be delayed?
Wie viel Verspätung wird es haben? (*vee*-feel fer-*shpate*-toong veird air har-ben)

TRAIN/RAILWAY
ZUG/EISENBAHN

Where is the railway station?
Wo ist der Bahnhof? (*voh* ist der *barn*-hof)

departure
Abfahrt (*up*-fart)

arrival
Ankunft (*arn*-koonft)

Which platform?
Welcher Bahnsteig? (*vel*-kher *barn*-shtike)

A ... ticket please
Eine ... Fahrkarte bitte (ine ... *far*-car-te bitter)

◆ **single**
◆ einfache Fahrkarte (*ine*-fukh-er *far*-car-te)

◆ **return**
◆ Rückfahrkarte (rook-far-car-te)

◆ **child's**
◆ Kinderfahrkarte (*kin*-der-far-car-te)

◆ **1st class**
◆ erste Klasse (*ers*-ter *cluss*-ser)

- **2nd class**
- zweite Klasse
  (*tsvy*-ter *cluss*-ser)

- **non-smoking**
- Nichtraucher
  (*nikht*-row-kher)

**Do I have to pay
a supplement?**
Muss ich einen Zuschlag
zahlen? (*mousse ikh inen
tsoo*-shlarg *tsar*-len)

**Is my ticket valid on
this train?**
Ist meine Fahrarte gültig
für diesen Zug? (*ist my-
ne far*-car-te *gool*-tig
foor *dee*-zen *tsoog*)

Do I have to change?
Muss ich umsteigen?
(*mousse ikh oom*-shty-
gen)

**Where do I have to
get off?**
Wo muss ich aussteigen?
(*voh mousse ikh ous*-
shty-gen)

**Do you have a
timetable?**
Haben Sie einen
Fahrplan? (*har-ben zee
inen far*-plarn)

I want to book ...
Ich möchte ... buchen
(*ikh mur'kh-te ... boo-
khen*)

- **a seat**
- einen Platz (Sitzplatz)
  (*inen pluts [seets*-pluts])

Is this seat free?
Ist dieser Platz frei? (*ist
dee-zer pluts fry*)

**May I open (close)
the window?**
Darf ich das Fenster auf-
machen (zumachen)?
(*darf ikh dos fens*-ter *ouf-
mar-khen (tsoo*-mar-
khen)

> **ICE INTERCITY
> EXPRESS
> (SUPPLEMENT)**
> EC/IC
> EUROCITY/INTERCITY
> (ZUSCHLAG)

**information and
tickets, information
office**
Auskunft und Fahrkarten,
Reisezentrum
(*ous*-koonft oont *far*-car-
ten, *rye-ze-cent*-room)

platform indicator
Gleisanzeiger (*glice-arn-tsai-ger*)

left luggage lockers
Schliessfächer (*shleece-fe'kher*)

stationmaster
Stationsvorsteher (*shtar-tsee-ions-for-shtay-er*)

What station is this?
Welcher Bahnhof ist das? (*vel-kher barn-hof ist dos*)

BOATS
DAMPFER/SCHIFFE/BOOTE

cruise
Kreuzfahrt (*croyts-fart*)

Can we hire a boat?
Können wir ein Boot mieten? (*cur-nen veer ine bort mee-ten*)

How much is a round trip?
Wieviel kostet eine Rund-fahrt? (*vee-feel koss-tet ine roond-fart?*)

one ticket
eine Fahrkarte (*ine far-car-te*)

two tickets
zwei Fahrkarten (*tsvy far-car-ten*)

How long is the trip?
Wie lange dauert die Fahrt? (*vee lung-ge dow'ert dee fart*)

Can we eat on board?
Können wir an Bord essen? (*cur-nen veer un bort es-sen*)

When is the last boat?
Wann geht das letzte Schiff? (*vann gait dos lets-te shiff*)

When is the next ferry?
Wann geht die nächste Fähre? (*vann gait dee nex-te fair-rer*)

Is the sea rough?
Ist hoher Seegang? (*ist hoh-er zay-gung*)

I feel seasick
Mir ist schlecht (*meer ist shlekht*)

TAXI
TAXI

Please order me a taxi
Bitte bestellen Sie mir ein Taxi (*bitter bay-shtel-len zee meer ein taxi*)

Where can I get a taxi?
Wo finde ich ein Taxi? (*voh fynn-de ikh ine taxi*)

To this address, please
Zu dieser Adresse bitte (*tsoo dee-zer ard-ress-se bitter*)

How much is it to the city centre?
Was kostet eine Fahrt ins Stadtzentrum? (*vos cuss-tet ine fart eens shtart-tsen-troom*)

To the airport, please
Zum Flughafen bitte (*tsoom floog-har-fen bitter*)

How much will it cost?
Wieviel kostet es? (*vee-feel kors-tet es*)

To the station, please
Zum Bahnhof bitte (*Tsoom barn-hof bitter*)

Keep the change
Stimmt so (*Shtimmt zoh*)

I need a receipt
Ich brauche eine Quittung (*Ikh brow-khe ine quit-toong*)

AIRPORT
FLUGHAFEN

arrival
Ankunft (*arn-koonft*)

departure
Abflug (*arp-floog*)

flight number
Flugnummer (*floog-noom-mer*)

delay
Verspätung (*fer-shpay-toong*)

check-in
Abfertigung (*arp-fair too goong*)

hand luggage
Handgepäck (*harnd-gay-pack*)

boarding card
Bordkarte (*bort-car-te*)

gate
Flugsteig (*floog-shtike*)

last call
letzter Aufruf (*lets-ter ouf-roof*)

valid, invalid
gültig, ungültig (*gool-tig, oon-gool-tig*)

baggage/luggage claim
Gepäckausgabe (*gay-peck-ous-garb-be*)

lHow can I get to town?
Wie komme ich in die Stadt? (*vee kom-me ikh in dee shtard*)

Where do I get the bus to the centre?
Wo ist der Bus zum Zentrum? (*voh ist der boos tsoom cent-room*)

Where do I check in for ... ?
Wo muss ich einchecken für ... ? (*voh moousse ikh ine-shek-ken foor ...*)

An aisle/window seat, please
Bitte einen Gangplatz/Fensterplatz (*bitter inen gung-plats/fence-ter-plats*)

Where is the gate for the flight to ... ?
Wo ist der Flugsteig für ... ? (*voh ist der floog-styg foor ...*)

I have nothing to declare
Ich habe nichts zu verzollen (*ikh har-be nix tsoo fer-tsol-len*)

It's for my own personal use
Es ist für meinen persönlichen Gebrauch (*ass ist foor mine-en per-zoon-lee-khen gay-brow'kh*)

The flight has been cancelled
Der Flug ist gestrichen (*der fluke ist gay-shtree-khen*)

The flight has been delayed
Der Flug ist verschoben (*der fluke ist fer-shore-ben*)

ROAD TRAVEL/ CAR HIRE
AUTOFAHRTEN/ AUTOVERMIETUNG

Have you got a road map?
Haben Sie eine Strassen-karte? (*har-ben zee ine shtross-sen-car-te*)

How many kilo-metres is it to ... ?
Wieviele Kilometer sind es bis ... ?
(*vee-feeler keel-lo-metre synd es biss ...*)

Where is the nearest garage?
Wo ist die nächste Tankstelle? (*voh ist dee nex-te tarnk-shtel-le*)

Fill it up, please
Bitte volltanken (*bitter foll-tarn-ken*)

Please check the oil, water, battery and tyres
Bitte prüfen Sie Öl, Wasser, Batterie und Reifen (*bitter proo-fen zee url, vas-ser, but-ter-ree oond rye-fen*)

I'd like to hire a car
Ich möchte ein Auto mieten (*ikh mur'kh-te ine ow-tore mee-ten*)

How much does it cost per week/day?
Wieviel kostet es pro Woche/Tag? (*vee-feel kors-tet es proh vore-khe/targ*)

What do you charge per kilometre?
Was nehmen Sie pro Kilometer? (*vos nay-men zee proh kee-lo-metre*)

Is the mileage unlimited?
Ist die Kilometerzahl unbegrenzt? (*ist dee kee-lo-metre-tsarl oon-be-gren-sed*)

Where can I pick up the car?
Wo bekomme ich den Wagen? (*voh bay-kom-me ikh den var-gen*)

Where can I leave the car?
Wo gebe ich den Wagen ab? (*voh gay-be ikh den var-gen arp*)

garage
Garage, Tankstelle,
Werkstatt (car repairs)
(*ga-rahr-jer, tunk-shtel-le,
vegg-shtatt*)

headlight
Scheinwerfer
(*shine-ver-fair*)

engine
Motor (*moh-tore*)

windscreen
Windschutzscheibe
(*vind-shoots-shye-be*)

**What is the speed
limit?**
Was ist die Höchst-
geschwindigkeit?
(*voss ist die ur'khst-gay-
shveen-deeg-kite*)

**The keys are locked
in the car**
Die Schlüssel sind im
Auto eingeschlossen
(*dee shlew-sel zeend im
ow-tore ine-gay-shlos-
sen*)

**The engine is
overheating**
Der Motor ist heiss-
gelaufen. (*der moh-tore
ist hice-gay-low-fen*)

Have you got ... ?
Haben Sie ... ?
(*har-ben zee ...*)

◆ **a towing rope**
◆ ein Abschleppseil
  (*ine arp-shlepp-zile*)

◆ **a spanner**
◆ einen Schrauben
  schlüssel (*ine-nen
  shrow-ben-shlews-sel*)

> **ROAD SIGNS**
> VERKEHRSZEICHEN

No through road
Durchfahrt verboten
(*door'kh-fart fer-bor-ten*)

one-way street
Einbahnstrasse
(*ine-barn-shtrar-sse*)

entrance
Eingang, Einfahrt
(*ine-gung, ine-fart*)

exit
Ausgang, Ausfahrt
(*ous-gung, ous-fart*)

**Keep the entrance
clear**
Eingang freihalten
(*ine-gung fry-hul-ten*)

Residents only
Für Anlieger frei (foor _arn_-leaguer _fry_)

pedestrians
Fussgänger (_fousse_-gang-er)

danger
Gefahr (gay-_far_)

speed limit
Geschwindigkeitsbe-grenzung (gay-_shveen_-dig-kites-be-_grence_-oong)

No entry
Kein Eingang (kine _ine_-gung)

roundabout
Kreisverkehr (_crice_-fer-care)

Insert coins
Münzen einwerfen (_moon_-zen _ine_-ver-fen)

Returned coins
Münzrückgabe (moonce-_rurk_-gar-be)

No parking
Parken verboten (_par_-ken fer-_bore_-ten)

cul de sac
Sackgasse (_zuk_-gus-se)

car park
Parkplatz (_park_-pluts)

supervised car park
Überwachter Parkplatz (oo-ber-_vakh_-ter _park_-pluts)

No right turn
Rechts abbiegen verboten (re'khts _arp_-bee-gen fer-_bore_-ten)

detour
Umleitung (_oom_-lite-toong)

No admission for unauthorized persons
Unbefugten ist der Zutritt verboten (_oon_-bay-foog-ten ist der _tsoo_-tritt fer-_bore_-ten)

No stopping
Halteverbot (_harl_-te fer-bort)

No overtaking
Überholverbot (oo-ber-_horl_-fer-bort)

Toll
Zollstelle (tsöll-shtel-le)

roadworks
Strassenarbeiten (_shtrus_-sen-arb-_bye_-ten)

ACCOMMODATION
UNTERKUNFT

Bed & Breakfast
Frühstückspension
(*froo*-shtooks-
pen-zee-*on*)

Vacancies
Zimmer frei
(*tsim*-mer fry)

Have you a room ... ?
Haben Sie ein Zimmer ... ?
(*har*-ben zee ine *tsim*-
mer)

◆ **for tonight**
◆ für heute Nacht
  (foor hoyte nakht)

◆ **with breakfast**
◆ mit Frühstück
  (mit *froo*-shtook)

◆ **room only**
◆ ohne Frühstück
  (*or*-ne *froo*-shtook)

◆ **with bath**
◆ mit Bad
  (mit bard)

◆ **with shower**
◆ mit Dusche
  (mit *doo*-sher)

◆ **single room**
◆ Einzelzimmer
  (*ine*-tsel-tsim-mer)

◆ **double room**
◆ Doppelzimmer
  (*dop*-pel-tsim-mer)

◆ **family room**
◆ Familienzimmer (fam-
  me-lyon-tsim-mer)

**How much is the
room ... ?**
Wieviel kostet das
Zimmer ... ? (*vee*-feal
cost-ted dass *tsim*-mer)

◆ **per day**
◆ pro Tag (pro *targ*)

◆ **per week**
◆ pro Woche
  (pro *vo*'kher)

**Have you got
anything cheaper/
better?**
Haben sie etwas
Billigeres/Besseres?
(*har*-ben zee et-vass *bil*-
lig-ger-res/*bess*-ser-ress

May I see the room?
Kann ich das Zimmer
ansehen? (*cahn* ikh dass
tsim-mer *arn*-zain)

Do you have a cot?
Haben Sie ein
Kinderbett? *(har-ben zee
ine kin-der-bett)*

**What time is
breakfast/dinner?**
Wann gibt es Frühstück/
Abendessen? *(vann
geebt ess froo-shtook /
ar-bend-ess-sen)*

room service
Zimmerservice, Zimmer-
dienst *(tsim-mer-zer-
veez, tsim-mer-deenst)*

Please bring ...
Bringen Sie bitte ...
(bring-gen zee ... bitter)

♦ **toilet paper**
♦ Toilettenpapier
  (toy-let-ten-pa-peer)

♦ **clean towels**
♦ saubere Handtücher
  *(zow-be-re harnd-
  too-kher)*

Please clean ...
Machen Sie bitte ...
sauber *(mar'khen-zee
bitter ... zow-ber)*

♦ **the bath**
♦ das Bad *(dass bard)*

**Please put fresh
sheets on the bed**
Bitte beziehen sie das
Bett frisch *(bitter bay-
tseen zee dass bett frish)*

Please don't touch ...
Bitte fassen Sie nicht ... an
*(bitter farce-cen zee
neekht ... arn)*

♦ **my briefcase**
♦ meine Aktentasche
  (miner arc-ten-tar-she)

♦ **my laptop**
♦ mein Laptop
  (mine laptop)

My ... doesn't work
Mein/e ... funktioniert
nicht *(mine/miner ...
foonk-tseeoo-neert
ni'kht)*

♦ **toilet**
♦ Toilette *(toy-let-te)*

♦ **bedside lamp**
♦ Nachttischlampe
  (narkh-tish-larm-pe)

**There is no hot
water**
Es gibt kein heisses
Wasser *(ess geept kain
high-cess vos-ser)*

RECEPTION
EMPFANG

Are there any messages for me?
Sind Nachrichten für mich da? *(zeend nar'kh-reekh-ten foor mikh dahr)*

Has anyone asked for me?
Hat jemand nach mir gefragt? *(hot yay-mond nar'kh meer gay-frahgt)*

Can I leave a message for someone?
Kann ich eine Nachricht für jemand hinterlassen? *(carn ikh iner nakh-rikht hin-ter-las-sen)*

Is there a laundry service?
Gibt es einen Wäsche-service? *(geept ess inen ve-sher-ser-viss)*

I need a wake-up call at 7 o'clock
Ich möchte um 7 Uhr geweckt werden *(ikh mur'kh-te oom zee-ben oor gay-vekt ver-den)*

What number must I dial for room service?
Welche Nummer muss ich für Zimmerservice wählen? *(vel-khe noo-mer mousse ikh foor tsim-mer-ser-viss vay-len)*

Where is the lift/elevator?
Wo ist der Fahrstuhl / Aufzug? *(voh ist der far-shtool / owf-tsoog)*

Do you arrange tours?
Organisieren Sie Rundfahrten? *(or-ghan-nee-zee-ren zee roond-fart-ten)*

Please prepare the bill
Machen Sie bitte die Rechnung fertig *(mar'khen zee bitter die rekh-noong fair-teeg)*

There is a mistake in the bill
Da ist ein Fehler in der Rechnung *(dahr ist ine fair-ler in der rekh-noong)*

I'm leaving tomorrow
Ich reise morgen ab *(ikh ray-ze mor-gen arp)*

SELF-CATERING
SELBSTVERSORGUNG

Have you any vacancies?
Ist noch etwas frei?
(ist nokh et-vass fry)

How much is it per night/week?
Was kostet es pro Nacht / Woche? *(vos cuss-ded ess pro nakht / vor-kher)*

How big is it?
Wie gross ist es?
(vee gross ist ess)

Do you allow children?
Sind Kinder auch gestattet? *(zind kin-der auch gay-shtut-tet)*

Please, show me how ... works
Bitte zeigen Sie mir, wie ... funktioniert *(bitter tsai-gen zee meer, vee ... foonk-tseeoo-neert)*

◆ **the cooker/stove, oven**
◆ der Herd, Ofen
(der haird, oh-fen)

◆ **the washing machine**
◆ die Waschmaschine
(dee vash-ma-shee-ne)

◆ **the dryer**
◆ der Trockner
(der trock-ner)

◆ **the hair-dryer**
◆ der Fön *(der furn)*

◆ **the heater**
◆ die Heizung
(dee hite-tsoong)

◆ **the water heater**
◆ das Heisswassergerät, der Boiler *(dos hice-vos-ser-gay-rate, der boiler)*

Where is/are ... ?
Wo ist/sind ... ?
(voh ist/zind ...)

◆ **the switch**
◆ der Schalter
(der shull-ter)

◆ **the fuses**
◆ die Sicherungen
(dee zi'khe-roon-gen)

Is there ... ?
Gibt es ... ? *(geept ess ...)*

- **a cot**
- ein Kinderbett
  (ine <u>kin</u>-der-bet)

- **a high chair**
- einen Kinderstuhl
  (inen <u>kin</u>-der-stool)

- **a safe**
- ein Safe *(inen safe)*

We need more ...
Wir brauchen mehr ...
(veer <u>brow</u>-khen <u>mare</u> ...)

- **cutlery**
- Besteck *(bay-<u>shteck</u>)*

- **crockery**
- Geschirr *(gay-<u>sheer</u>)*

- **sheets**
- Bettwäsche
  (bett-<u>vay</u>-she)

- **blankets**
- Decken *(<u>deck</u>-en)*

- **pillows**
- Kopfkissen
  (<u>kopf</u>-kiss-sen)

Is there ... in the vicinity?
Gibt es ... in der Nähe?
(geept ess .... in der <u>nay</u>-er)

- **a restaurant**
- ein Restaurant
  (ine res-tow-<u>runt</u>)

- **a bus, tram**
- einen Bus, eine Strassenbahn *(inen boos, ine <u>shtras</u>-sen-barn)*

We would like to stay for ...
Wir möchten für ... bleiben
(veer mur'kh-ten foor ... <u>bly</u>-ben)

- **three nights**
- drei Nächte
  (dry <u>nair'kh</u>-te)

- **one week**
- eine Woche
  (ine <u>vo</u>'kher)

I have locked myself out
Ich habe mich ausgesperrt *(ikh <u>har</u>-be meekh <u>ows</u>-gay-shpairred*

The window won't open/close
Das Fenster lässt sich nicht öffnen/ schliessen *(dos <u>fen</u>-stir lest si'kh ni'kht <u>urf</u>-nen/<u>shlee</u>-sen)*

CAMPING
ZELTEN

Caravan
Wohnwagen
(*vaughn-var-gen*)

Have you got a list of campsites?
Haben Sie eine Liste mit Campingplätzen? (*harben zee iner lis-te mit camping-plet-sen*)

Are there any sites available?
Sind noch Plätze frei? (*synd no'kh plet-se fry*)

How much is it per night/week?
Was kostet es pro Nacht/Woche? (*vos kors-ted ess pro nakht/vor'khe*)

Can we park the caravan here?
Können wir den Wohnwagen hier parken? (*cur-nen veer den vaughn-war-gen here par-ken*)

Is there electricity?
Gibt es Strom? (*geept ess shtrohm*)

Can we camp here overnight?
Können wir über Nacht hier zelten? (*cur-nen veer oo-ber nakht heer tsel-ten*)

This site is very muddy
Dieser Platz ist sehr schlammig (*dee-zer plats ist zer shlum-meeg*)

Is there a sheltered site?
Gibt es einen geschützten Platz? (*geept ess inen gay-shoots-ten plats*)

Is there ... in the vicinity?
Gibt es ... in der Nähe? (*geept ess ... in der nay-er*)

◆ **a shop**
◆ einen Laden
  (*inen lar-den*)

◆ **a restaurant**
◆ ein Restaurant
  (*ine ress-tow-runt*)

◆ **an eating place**
◆ eine Gaststätte
  (*ine gust-stay-te*)

- **a garage**
- eine Tankstelle
  (iner <u>tunk</u>-shtel-le)

We would like to stay for ...
Wir möchte für ...
bleiben *(veer mur'kh-ten foor ... <u>bly</u>-ben)*

- **three nights**
- drei Nächte
  (<u>dry</u> nekh-te)

- **one week**
- eine Woche
  (iner <u>vor</u>-khe)

Is there drinking water?
Gibt es Trinkwasser?
(geept ess <u>trink</u>-vos-ser)

Can I light a fire here?
Kann man hier ein Feuer machen? *(kon mon heer <u>foyer</u> <u>mar</u>-khen)*

I'd like to buy fire wood
Ich möchte Brennholz kaufen *(ikh <u>mur</u>'khte <u>brenn</u>-holts <u>oow</u> fen*

Is the wood dry?
Ist das Holz trocken? *(ist duss holts <u>trock</u>-ken)*

Do you have ... for rent?
Haben Sie ... zu vermieten? *(har-ben zee ... tsoo fer-<u>mee</u>-ten*

- **a tent**
- ein Zelt *(ine tselt)*

- **a gas cylinder**
- eine Gasflasche
  (iner <u>gus</u>-flusher)

- **a groundsheet**
- eine Zeltbodenplane
  (iner <u>tselt</u>-bor-den-<u>plar</u>-ne)

- **cooking utensils**
- Kochgeräte
  (kokh-gay-<u>rate</u>-ter)

Where is the nearest ... ?
Wo ist der/das nächste ...
(voh ist der/duss nerkh-ste ...)

- **toilet block**
- Toilettenblock
  (toy-<u>let</u>-ten-block)

- **sink (for washing dishes)**
- Abwaschbecken
  (<u>arp</u>-vush-<u>beck</u>-ken)

CUTLERY
BESTECK

knife
Messe (*mess-er*)

fork, cake fork
Gabel, Kuchengabel (*gar-bell, koo-khen-gar-bell*)

spoon, teaspoon
Löffel, Teelöffel (*lur-fell*), *tay-lur-fell*)

crockery
Geschirr (*gay-sheer*)

plate
Teller (*tell-er*)

cup and saucer, mug
Tasse und Untertasse, Becher (*tuss-er oont oon-ter-tuss-er, be-kher*)

BREAKFAST
FRÜHSTÜCK

coffee
Kaffee (*cuff-fe*)

◆ **black**
◆ schwarz (*shvarts*)

◆ **with milk, cream**
◆ mit Milch, Kaffeesahne (*mit milkh, cuff-fe-zar-ne*)

◆ **without sugar**
◆ ohne Zucker (*or-ne tsoo-ker*)

tea
Tee *tay*

◆ **with milk, lemon**
◆ mit Milch, Zitrone (*mit milkh, tsee-troh-ne*)

bread
Brot (*brought*)

rolls
Brötchen, Semmel (in the south) (*broit-khen, zemm-el*)

egg(s)
Ei/Eier (*eye/eye-er*)

◆ **boiled – soft, hard**
◆ gekocht – weich, hart (*gay-kokht – vaikh, hart*)

◆ **fried**
◆ Spiegelei (*shpoogle-eye*)

◆ **scrambled**
◆ Rührei (*roor-eye*)

◆ **poached**
◆ poschiertes
   (pore-sheer-tes)

bacon and eggs
Eier mit Speck
(eyer mit shpeck)

cereal
Getreideflocken
(gay-try-der-flok-ken)

hot milk, cold milk
heisse Milch, kalte Milch
(heis-ser milkh, cull-ter milkh)

fruit
Früchte *(frookh-te)*

orange juice
Orangensaft
(or-rang-jen-zarft)

jam
Konfitüre, Marmelade
(con-fee-ture-ray, marm-may-lard-de)

marmalade
Orangenmarmelade
(or-rang-jen-marm-may-lard-de)

pepper and salt
Pfeffer und Salz *(pfef-fer und zarlts)*

LUNCH/DINNER MITTAGESSEN/ ABENDESSEN

Could we have a table ... ?
Können wir einen Tisch ... haben? *(curn-nen veer inen tish ... har-ben)*

◆ **outside**
◆ draussen *(drow-sen)*

◆ **inside**
◆ drinnen *(drin-nen)*

May I have ... please?
Kann ich bitte ... haben? *(kun ikh bitter ... har-ben)*

◆ **the menu**
◆ die Speisekarte
   (dee shpai-zer-car-te)

◆ **the wine list**
◆ die Weinkarte
   (dee vine-car-te)

◆ **the menu of the day**
◆ die Tageskarte
   (dee tar-ges-car-te)

◆ **starters**
◆ Vorspeisen
   (for-shpai-zen)

- **main course**
- Hauptgericht
  (_howpt_-gay-reekht)

- **dessert**
- Nachtisch (_nakh_-tish)

I'll take the set menu
Ich nehme das Tages-
menü (_ikh nay-mer dos_
tar-gess-may-new)

What is this?
Was ist das?
(_vos ist dos_)

**That is not what
I ordered**
Das habe ich nicht
bestellt (_dos har_-be ikh
nikht bersh-telled)

It's tough, cold, off
Das ist zäh, kalt, verdorben
(_dos ist tsay, carlt,_
fer-dor-ben)

**What do you
recommend?**
Was empfehlen Sie?
(_vos amp-fay_-len _zee_)

How much is it?
Was kostet es?/
Wieviel macht das?
(_vee-feel mu'kht dos_

**Can I have the bill
please?**
Kann ich bitte die
Rechnung haben? (_cun_
ikh bitter dee rekh-noong
harb-ben)

**We'd like to pay
separately**
Wir möchten getrennt
bezahlen (_veer mur'kh-ten_
gay-_trenned_ bay-_tsar_-len)

There is a mistake
Das stimmt nicht
(_dos shtimmed nikht_)

Thanks, that's for you
Danke, das ist für Sie
(_darn-ke, dos ist foor zee_)

Keep the change
Stimmt so
(_shtimmed zore_)

DRINKS
GETRÄNKE

**a beer/Pilsener –
large, small**
ein Bier/Pils – gross, klein
(Krügl/Seidel in Bavaria
and Austria)
(_ine beer/pills – grohss,_
kline [kroogle/sidle])

top-fermented beers
Altbier, Kölsch (mainly in Rhineland) *(arlt-beer, curlsh)*

bottom-fermented beers
Bockbier, Weihnachtsbier (festive beers) *(bock-beer, veye-nakhts-beer)*

low alcohol sweet stout
Malzbier *(malts-beer)*

wheat beer
Weizenbier *(vie-tsen-beer)*

draught beer
Fassbier *(farce-beer)*

a glass (¼ litre) of cider
ein Glas (ein Viertel) Apfelwein *(ine glass [ine feer-tel] arp-fel-vine)*

shandy
Alsterwasser (north), Radler (south) *(arl-ster-vuss-ser, rahd-ler)*

a glass of wine with soda water
eine Weinshorle *(ine vine-shore-le)*

a dry (sweet) white wine
einen trockenen (lieblichen) Weisswein *(inen trock-nen (leeb-li'khen) vice-vine)*

a light (full-bodied) red wine
einen leichten (voll-mundigen) Rotwein *(inen lie'kh-ten (foll-moon-dee-gen) roht-vine)*

new wine
Federweisser, Heuriger (Austria) *(fe-der-vie-sser, hoy-ree-ger)*

wine made from grapes after frost
Eiswein *(ice-vine)*

house wine
Hauswein (offener Wein in Austria) *(house-vine)*

punch
Bowle *(bor-le)*

red wine punch with flamed rum
Feuerzangenbowle *(foyer-tsung-gen-bor-le)*

mulled wine
Glühwein *(glue-vine)*

a brandy
einen Cognac, Weinbrand
(inen con-yak, vine-brunt)

whisky with/out ice
Whisky mit/ohne Eis
(viss-key mit/or-ne ice)

clear spirits (cereal)
Schnaps, Korn

clear spirits (fruit)
Obstler *(orbst-ler)*

**a mineral water –
still, sparkling**
ein Mineralwasser – still,
sprudelnd *(ine minner-
rahl-vass-ser – shtill,
shproodl'nt)*

**fruit juice, tomato
juice**
Fruchtsaft, Tomatensaft
*(frookht-zarft, tore-mar-
ten-zarft)*

another ... please
noch ein ... bitte *(no'kh
ine ... bitter)*

too cold
zu kalt *(tsoo carlt)*

not cold enough
nicht kalt genug *(nikht
carlt gay-nook)*

FOOD
SPEISEN

SOUP, CREAM SOUP
SUPPE, RAHMSUPPE
(zoo-pe, rahm-zoo-pe)

**potato soup, mush-
room soup**
Kartoffelsuppe, Pilzsuppe
*(car-to-fill-zoo-pe, pills-
zoo-pe)*

pea, lentil, bean soup
Erbsen-, Linsen-, Bohnen-
suppe *(airb-sen-, lynne-
sen-, bore-nen-zoo-pe)*

consommé
Kraftbrühe *(cruft-broo'er)*

FISH
FISCH *(fish)*

sole
Seezunge *(zay-tsoon-ge)*

plaice
Flunder *(floon-der)*

cod
Kabeljau, Dorsch *(car-bill-
yow, dorsh)*

salmon
Lachs *(lux)*

herring
Hering (*hehr*-ring)

trout
Forelle (for-*rel*-le)

tuna
Thunfisch (*toon*-fish)

fried, grilled, sautéed
gebraten, gegrillt,
gedünstet (*gay-bra*-ten,
gay-grilled, gay-*doons*-tet)

POULTRY
GEFLÜGEL (*gay-flew*-gill)

chicken
Huhn (*hoon*)

crumbed roasted chicken
paniertes Hühnerschnitzel
(Backhendl in the south)
(par-*neer*-tez *hoo*-ner-
shnit-sel, *buck*-handle)

duck
Ente (*en*-te)

goose
Gans (*gunts*)

roasted, grilled, fried
im Ofen gebacken, gegrillt,
gebraten (eem *ore*-fen
gay-*buck*-ken, gay-
grilled, gay-*bra*-ten)

MEAT
FLEISCH (*flysh*)

veal
Kalbfleisch (*culp*-flysh)

mutton, lamb
Hammelfleisch,
Lammfleisch (*hum*-mel-
flysh, *lum*-flysh)

beef
Rindfleisch (*rint*-flysh)

pork
Schweinefleisch
(shvaine-ne-flysh)

sausage, veal sausage
Bratwurst, Kalbsbratwurst
(*braht*-voorst, *culps*-
braht-voorst)

vienna, frankfurter
Wiener (Würstchen),
Bockwurst (*vee*-ner
voorst-khen, *bock*-voorst)

venison
Wild (*vilt*-flysh)

meat balls/cakes
Frikadellen, Klopse,
Bouletten, Fleischlaberl
(Austria) (free-car-*del*-len,
klop-se, *flysh*-lar-berl)

crumbed escalopes
Wiener Schnitzel
(*vee-*ner *shnit-*sel)

well done, medium, rare
durchgebraten, mittel, rot
(*dour'kh-gay-*bra-*ten, mit-tel, wrought*)

boiled, stewed
gekocht, gedünstet (*gay-ko'kht, gay-*doonz*-ted*)

brawn, aspic
Sülze, Sulz (Austria)
(*zool-*tse, zoolts*)

platter of cold meats
Kalte Platte, Aufschnitt
(*carl-*te *plart-*te, *owf-*shneet*)

blood polony
Blutwurst (*bloote-*voorst*)

pork, pickled and smoked
Kassler (*kuss-*ler*)

bacon
Schinken, Speck,
(*shcon* kon, *shpeck*)

PASTA, RICE, ETC.
NUDELN, REIS, USW.
(*noodeln, rice*)

dumplings
Klösse (north), Knödel (south) (*clurs-*se, *cnurdle*)

dumplings with apricots
Marillenknödel (Austria)
(*mar-*rill*-len-*cnurdle*)

pasta
Nudeln, Spätzle (south)
(*noodeln, shpets-*le*)

pasta made with cottage cheese
Topfennudeln (Austria)
(*top-*fen-noodeln*)

VEGETABLES, FRUIT AND SALAD
GEMÜSE, OBST UND SALAT
(*gay-*moo*-zer, orbst, zar-*lard*)

pickled white cabbage
Sauerkraut (*sour-*crowt*)

red cabbage
Rotkohl (north), Blaukraut (south) (*wrought-*kohl, *blou-*crowt*)

cauliflower
Blumenkohl
(*blue-*men-kohl*)

carrots
Karotten, Möhren (north)
(*car-_rot_-ten, _mur_-ren*)

asparagus
Spargel (*_shpurg_-gel*)

mushrooms
Pilze, Schwammerln
(Austria and Bavaria)
(*_pill_-se, _shvum_-merln*)

peppers
Paprika (*_pa_-pree-ker*)

**potatoes – boiled,
fried, mashed**
Kartoffeln – Salzkartoffeln,
Röst-/Bratkartoffeln, Püree
(*car-_toff_-eln – zults-, rost-,
braht-car-toff-eln, _pooh_-
ray*)

lettuce
Kopfsalat (*_korpf_-zar-lard*)

cucumbers
Gurken (*_goor_-ken*)

tomatoes
Tomaten (*tore-_mar_-ten*)

green beans
Grühne Bohnen
(*_grew_-ne bore-nen*)

apples
Äpfel (*_ep_-fell*)

pears
Birnen (*_beer_-nen*)

bananas
Bananen (*bar-_naa_-nen*)

pineapple
Ananas (*aa-naa-nuss*)

apricots
Aprikosen, Marillen (Austria)
(*up-ree-_co_-zen, ma-_rill_-en*)

peaches
Pfirsiche (*_fear_-zee-khe*)

lemon
Zitrone (*tsee-_troh_-ne*)

blueberries
Blaubeeren (*_blou_-bear-en*)

strawberries
Erdbeeren (*_aired_-bear-en*)

raspberries
Himbeeren (*_him_-bear-en*)

redcurrants
rote Johannisbeeren
(*_wrought_-te yo-_har_-nis-
bear-en*)

blackcurrants
schwarze
Johannisbeeren
(*_shvar_-tse yo-_har_-nis-
bear-en*)

plums, prunes
Zwetschgen**,**
Backpflaumen (*pflow-men*, *buck*-pflow-men)

fruit salad
Obst/Fruchtsalat
(*orbst*/*frookht*-zar-lard)

CAKES
KUCHEN

meringue
Baiser (*bay-zéh*)

marble cake
Marmorkuchen
(*mar*-more-koo-khen)

pastry with apples and raisins
Apfelstrudel
(*arp*-fel-stroodle)

doughnut
Berliner – jam-filled (north and south), Krapfen – unfilled (south)
(*bear-lee-ner*, *krah*-pfen)

Madeira cake
Sandkuchen
(*zund*-koo-khen)

fruit flan
Obstkuchen
(*orbst*-koo-khen)

gateau with cherries and cream
Schwarzwälder Kirsch-torte (*shvarts*-vel-der-*keersh*-tor-te)

light fruitcake in ring form
Guglhupf, Rosinenkuchen
(*google*-hoopf, roh-*zee*-nen-koo-khen)

plain cake with crumble topping
Streuselkuchen
(*shtroy*-zel-koo-khen)

gateau with nuts and butter icing
Nusstorte (*nousse*-tor-te)

poppyseed cake
Mohnkuchen
(*morn*-koo-khen)

honey and almond tart
Bienenstich
(*bee*-nen-shtikh)

sponge cake with chocolate
Sachertorte
(*sakh*-kher tor te)

raspberry jam flan
Linzertorte
(*lynne*-tser-tor-te)

MONEY MATTERS
GELDSACHEN

bureau de change
Geldwechsel (*gelt-vexle*)

cash dispenser/ATM
Geldautomat (*gelt-out-to-mart*)

Where can I change money?
Wo kann ich Geld wechseln? (*voh carn ikh gelt vexlen*)

Where is ... ?
Wo ist ... ? (*voh ist*)

♦ **an ATM, a bureau de change, a bank**
♦ ein Geldautomat, eine Wechselstube, eine Bank (*ine gelt-out-to-mart, ine vexle-shtoo-be, ine bunk*)

When does the bank open/close?
Wann macht die Bank auf/zu? (Wann öffnet/schliesst die Bank?) *vun mu'kht dee bunk ouf/tsoo vun urf-net/shleesst dee bunk)*

How much commission do you charge?
Wie hoch ist die Gebühr/-Kommission? (*vee hor'kh ist dee gay-bewer*)

I want to ...
Ich möchte ...
(*ikh mur'khte ...*)

♦ **cash a traveller's cheque**
♦ einen Reisescheck einlösen (*inen rye-zer-sheck ine-loo-zen*)

♦ **change £50**
♦ fünfzig Pfund wechseln (*foonf-tsig pfoond vexlen*)

♦ **make a transfer, remittance**
♦ eine Überweisung machen (*iner oober-vie-zoong mur'khen*)

POST OFFICE
POSTAMT

How much is ... ?
Was kostet ... ?
(*vahs kors-tet*)

- a letter to ...
- ein Brief nach ...
  (ine _breef_ nar'kh ...)

- a small parcel to ...
- ein Päckchen nach ...
  (ine _peck_-khen nakh ...)

Where can I buy stamps?
Wo kann ich Briefmarken kaufen? (voh kan ikh _breef_-mar-ken _cow_-fen)

SHOPPING
EINKAUFEN

What does it cost?
Was kostet das? (vahs _kors_-tet _duss_)

Where do I pay?
Wo zahle ich?
(voh _tsah_-le ikh)

I need a receipt
Ich brauche eine Quittung (ikh _brow_-khe ine _quit_-toong)

Do you accept credit cards?
Nehmen Sie Kreditkarten? (_nay_-men zee cre-_deet_-_cart_-ten)

Do you take traveller's cheques?
Nehmen Sie Reiseschecks? (_nay_-men zee _ry_-ze-shecks)

Does that include VAT?
Ist die Mehrwertsteuer inbegriffen? (ist dee _mare_-vert-shtoyer _in_-be-_grif_-fen)

VAT
MWS (Mehrwertsteuer)
(_mare_-vert-shtoyer)

Can you wrap it up for me?
Können Sie es für mich einpacken? (_cur_-nen zee ess foor mikh _ine_-puck-ken)

This isn't correct (bill)
Das stimmt nicht (dos _shteemt_ ni'kht)

This isn't what I want
Das ist nicht, was ich möchte (dos ist _nikht_ vos ikh _mur'kh_-te)

I want my money back
Ich möchte mein Geld zurück (haben) (ikh murkh-te mine _gelt_ tsoo-_rook_ [_har_-ben])

I want to complain
Ich möchte mich
beschweren *(ikh mur'kh-
te meekh bay-shvair-ren)*

This is ...
Das ist ... *(dos ist ...)*

- **broken**
- kaputt *(car-put)*

- **damaged**
- beschädigt
  (bay-shade-dikt)

- **old/stale**
- alt *(arlt)*

> **BUYING FOOD**
> LEBENSMITTEL
> KAUFEN

Where can I buy ... ?
Wo kann ich ... kaufen?
(voh kan ikh ... cow-fen)

- **bread**
- Brot *(broht)*

- **rolls**
- Brötchen/Semmeln
  (south) *(broid-khen/
  zem-meln)*

- **cheese**
- Käse *(kay-ze)*

- **butter**
- Butter *(boot-ter)*

- **milk**
- Milch *(mil'kh)*

- **water**
- Wasser *(vos-ser)*

- **wine**
- Wein *(vine)*

- **sparkling wine**
- Sekt *(zeckt)*

- **beer**
- Bier *(beer)*

- **fruit juice**
- Fruchtsaft
  (froo'kht-zuft)

- **meat**
- Fleisch *(flysh)*

- **ham**
- Schinken *(sheen-ken)*

- **polony/cold meats**
- Wurst, Aufschnitt
  (selection)
  (voorst, owf-shneet)

- **sausages**
- Würstchen (cooked),
  Bratwurst (for frying)
  (vurst-kheen, brat-vurst)

- **cake**
- Kuchen (_koo_-khen)

- **fruit**
- Obst (orbst)

- **vegetables**
- Gemüse (gay-_mew_-se)

- **eggs**
- Eier (_eye_-er)

I'll take ...
Ich nehme ...
(ikh nay-me ...)

- **one kilo**
- ein Kilo (ine _key_-low)

- **three slices**
- drei Scheiben
  (dry _shy_-ben)

- **a portion of**
- eine Portion
  (iner port-see-_on_)

- **a packet of**
- ein Paket (ine pah-_kayt_)

- **a can/tin of**
- eine Dose/Büchse
  (iner _doh_-ze/_boo_-xer)

- **a bottle of**
- eine Flasche
  (ine _flar_-sher)

BUYING CLOTHES
KLEIDUNG KAUFEN

Can I try this on?
Kann ich das anprobieren?
(carn ikh dos _am_-pro-
beer-ren)

It is too ...
Es ist zu ... (ess ist _tsoo_ ...)

- **big**
- gross (gross)

- **small**
- klein (kline)

- **tight**
- eng (ang)

- **wide**
- weit (vite)

- **expensive**
- teuer (_toy_-er)

- **fragile, delicate**
- zerbrechlich,
  empfindlich (tser-_bre'kh_-
  likh, em-_fiend_-likh)

I'll take ...
Ich nehme ...
(ikh _nay_-me ...)

- **this one**
- dieses (_dee_-zes)

CLOTHING SIZES – KLEIDERGRÖSSEN

Women's Wear

UK	Cont. Europe	USA
10	38	8
12	40	10
14	42	12
16	44	14
18	46	16

Menswear

UK	Cont. Europe	USA
36	46	36
38	48	38
40	50	40
42	52	42
44	54	44
46	56	46

Men's Shirts

UK	Cont. Europe	USA
14	36	14
14.5	37	14.5
15	38	15
15.5	39	15.5
16	40	16
17	42	17

Shoes

UK	Cont. Europe	USA
5	39	6
6	40	7
7	41	0
8	42	9
9	43	10
10	44	11
11	45	12

SIGHTSEEING
BESICHTIGUNGEN
MACHEN

Tourist Office
Fremdenverkehrsbüro
(*frem*-den-fer-*cares*-
bureau)

**Do you have
brochures/leaflets?**
Haben sie Broschüren?
(*harben zee bro-jure-ren*)

I/We want to visit ...
Ich/wir möchte/n ...
besuchen
(*ikh/veer mur'kh-te/n ...
bay-zoo-khen*)

**When is it
open/closed?**
Wann ist es geöffnet/
geschlossen? (*vunn ist
ess gay-urf-net/
gay-shlos-sen*)

What does it cost?
Wieviel kostet es?
(*vee-feel kors-tet es*)

**Are there any
reductions for ... ?**
Gibt es Ermässigungen
für ... ? (*geept ess er-may-
see-goon-gen foor ...*)

♦ **children**
♦ Kinder (*keen-der*)

♦ **senior citizens**
♦ Rentner (*rent-ner*)

♦ **students**
♦ Studenten
(*shtoo-den-ten*)

Are there any tours?
Gibt es Rundfahrten/
Ausflugsfahrten? (*geept
es roond-far-ten/ows-
floogs-far-ten*)

**When does the
coach/bus depart?**
Wann fährt der Bus ab?
(*vun fairt der boos arb*)

**When does the
coach/bus return?**
Wann kommt der Bus
zurück? (*vun kommt der
boos tsoo-rurk*)

**Where is the
museum?**
Wo ist das Museum? (*voh
ist dos moo-zay-oom*)

**How much is the
entrance fee?**
Was kostet der Eintritt?
(*vos kors-tet der ine-tritt*)

ENTERTAINMENT
VERANSTALTUNGEN

Is there a list of cultural events?
Gibt es einen Veranstaltungskalender?
(geept ess inen fer-<u>arn</u>-shtul-toongs-kah-<u>len</u>-der)

Are there any festivals?
Gibt es Festivals?
(geept ess festivals)

I would like to go to ...
Ich möchte in ... gehen
(ikh mur'kh-te ... gain)

- **the theatre**
- ins Theater
  (inns tay-ar-ter)

- **the opera**
- die Oper (dee oh-per)

- **the ballet**
- ins Ballett
  (inns bar-lett)

- **the cinema/movies**
- ins Kino
  (inns kee-no)

- **a concert**
- ein Konzert
  (ine kon-<u>tsert</u>)

Do I have to book?
Muss ich buchen?
(mousse ikh <u>boo</u>-khen)

How much are the tickets?
Was kosten die Karten?
(vos <u>kors</u>-ten dee <u>car</u>-ten)

Two tickets for ...
Zwei Karten für ...
(tsvy <u>car</u>-ten foor)

- **tonight**
- heute Abend
  (hoy-ter <u>ar</u>-bend)

- **tomorrow night**
- morgen Abend
  (<u>mor</u>-gen <u>ar</u>-bend)

- **the early show**
- die Frühvorstellung
  (fee <u>froo</u>-for-shtel-loong)

- **the late show**
- die Spätvorstellung
  (dee <u>shpate</u>-for-shtel-loong)

When does the performance start/end?
Wann beginnt/endet die Vorstellung? (vun bay-<u>geent</u>/<u>ain</u>-ded dee <u>for</u>-shtel-loong)

Where is ... ?
Wo ist ... ? *(voh ist ...)*

- **a good bar**
- eine gute Bar/Kneipe *(ine goo-te bar/cny-per)*

- **good live music**
- gute Live-Musik *(goo-te live moo-seek)*

Is it ... ?
Ist es ... ? *(ist ess ...)*

- **expensive**
- teuer *(toy-er)*

- **noisy**
- laut *(lout)*

- **crowded**
- voll *(foll)*

How do I get there?
Wie komme ich hin? *(vee kom-mer ikh heen)*

SPORT
SPORT

Where can we ... ?
Wo können wir ... ? *(voh cur-nen veer ...)*

- **go riding**
- reiten *(rye-ten)*

- **play tennis/golg=f**
- Tennis/Golf spielen *(tennis/golf shpee-len)*

- **go skiing**
- Skifahren *(shee-far-en)*

- **go swimming**
- schwimmen (indoors), baden (outdoors) *(shvim-men, bar-den)*

- **go fishing**
- angeln *(ung-geln)*

- **go cycling**
- Radfahren *(rard-far-en)*

- **hire bicycles**
- Fahrräder ausleihen *(far-raid-der ows-lye-en)*

- **hire tackle**
- Ausrüstung ausleihen *(ows-rurs-toong ows-ly-en)*

- **hire tennis rackets**
- Tennisschläger ausleihen *(tennis-shlay-ger ows-lye-en)*

- **hire golf clubs**
- Golfschläger ausleihen *(golf-shlay-ger ows-lye-en)*

- **hire skis**
- Skier ausleihen
  (_shee_-er _ows_-lye-en)

- **hire a boat**
- ein Boot mieten
  (ine _bort_ _mee_-ten)

- **hire skates**
- Schlittschuhe ausleihen
  (_shleet_-shoe-er
  ows-lye-en)

- **hire an umbrella**
- einen Schirm ausleihen
  (inen _sheerm_
  ows-lye-en)

- **hire a deck chair**
- einen Liegestuhl mieten
  (inen _lee_-ger-shtool
  mee-ten)

How much is it ... ?
Wieviel kostet es ... ?
(_vee_-feel _kors_-tet es ...)

- **per hour**
- pro Stunde
  (pro _shtoon_-der)

- **per day**
- pro Tag (pro targ)

- **per session/game**
- pro Runde/Spiel
  (pro _roon_-der/shpeel)

Is it ... ?
Ist es ... ? (ist ess ...)

- **safe**
- sicher (_see_-kher)

- **deep**
- tief _teef_

- **clean**
- sauber _zow-ber_

How do we get there?
Wie kommen wir hin?
(vee _kom_-men vir heen)

No swimming/diving
Baden/Tauchen verboten
(_bar_-den/_tow_-khen fer-_bore_-ten)

Are there currents?
Sind da Strömungen?
(zind dar _shtroo_-moon-gen)

Do I need a fishing permit?
Brauche ich einen Angelschein? (_brow_-khe eekh inen _arngle_-shine)

Where can I get one?
Wo bekomme ich einen?
(voh _bay_-korm-me ikh inen)

Is there a guide for walks?
Gibt es einen Wander-führer? (*geept ess inen von-der-foo-rer*)

Do I need walking boots?
Brauche ich Wanderstiefel? (*brow-khe eekh von-der-shtee-fel*)

How much is a ski pass?
Was kostet ein Skipass? (*wuss kors-tet ine shee-pus*)

Is there a map of the ski runs?
Gibt es eine Pistenkarte? (*geept ess iner pis-ten-car-te*)

Do you offer skiing lessons?
Bieten Sie Skikurse an? (*beat-ten zee shee-cour-se arn*)

I'm a beginner
Ich bin Anfänger (*ikh bin arn-feng-ger*)

Is there a ski lift?
Gibt es einen Skilift? (*geept ess inen shee-lift*)

My skis are too long/short
Meine Skier sind zu lang/kurz (*mine-ne shee-er zind tsoo lung/koorts*)

Run Closed
Piste gesperrt (*pis-te gay-shperrt*)

Avalanches
Lawinen (*lahr-vee-nen*)

We want to go ...
Wir möchten ... (*veer mur'kh-ten ...*)

♦ **hiking**
♦ Wandern (*vun-dern*)

♦ **canoeing**
♦ Kanu fahren (*canoe fah-ren*)

♦ **mountaineering**
♦ Bergsteigen (*bairg-shty-gen*)

♦ **sailing**
♦ Segeln (*zay-geln*)

♦ **ice-skating**
♦ Schlittschuhlaufen (*shleet-shoe-low-fen*)

♦ **water-skiing**
♦ Wasserski fahren (*vos-ser-shee fa-ren*)

PHARMACY/CHEMIST
APOTHEKE (red letter A on white sign)

Chains for toiletries, etc., and some medicines not on prescription
Drogerie (dro-ghe-_ree_)

Health shop
Reformhaus
(ray-_form_-house)

Have you got something for ... ?
Haben Sie etwas gegen ... ? (har-ben zee _ett_-vos _gay_-gen ...)

◆ **car sickness**
◆ Reisekrankheit
(_rye_-zer-krunk-hite)

◆ **diarrhoea**
◆ Durchfall (_doorkh_-fahl)

◆ **headache**
◆ Kopfschmerzen
(_kopf_-shmer-tsen)

◆ **a sore throat**
◆ Halsschmerzen
(_harls_-shmer-tsen)

◆ **nausea**
◆ Übelkeit (_ooble_-kite)

◆ **a cold, flu**
◆ Erkältung, Grippe
(er-_kel_-toong, _grip_-pe)

◆ **hay fever**
◆ Heuschnupfen
(_hoy_-shnoop-fen)

I need ...
Ich brauche ...
(ikh brow-khe ...)

◆ **indigestion tablets**
◆ Magentabletten
(_mar_-ghen-tub-_let_-ten)

◆ **laxative**
◆ Abführmittel
(_arp_-foor-mit-tel)

◆ **sleeping tablets**
◆ Schlaftabletten
(_shluf_-tub-_let_-ten)

◆ **painkillers**
◆ Schmerzmittel
(_shmerts_-mit-tel)

Is it safe for children?
Ist es auch für Kinder geeignet? (ist ess owkh foor _kyn_-der gay-_eye_-gnet)

I'm a diabetic
Ich bin Diabetiker *(ikh bin dee-ar-bay-tik-ker)*

I'm pregnant
Ich bin schwanger *(ikh bin shvung-ger)*

allergic
allergisch *(al-lerg-gish)*

DOCTOR
ARZT

I am ill
Ich bin krank *(ikh bin krahnk)*

I need a doctor
Ich brauche einen Arzt *(ikh brow-khe inen artst)*

He/she has a high temperature
Er/Sie hat hohes Fieber *(err/zee hot ho-hes fee-ber)*

It hurts
Es tut weh *(ess toot way)*

I'm going to be sick!
Ich muss mich übergeben! *(ikh mousse mikh oo-ber-gay-ben)*

Dentist
Zahnarzt *(tsarn-artst)*

I have toothache
Ich habe Zahnschmerzen *(ikh har-be tsarn-shmer-tsen)*

Ophthalmologist
Augenarzt *(ow-gen-artst)*

HOSPITAL
KRANKENHAUS

Will I have to go to hospital?
Muss ich ins Krankenhaus? *(mousse ikh ins krahn-ken-house)*

Where is the hospital?
Wo ist das Krankenhaus? *(voh ist duss krahn-ken-house)*

Which ward?
Welche Station? *(vel-khe shtar-tsee-oon)*

When are visiting hours?
Wann ist Besuchszeit? *(varn ist bay-zookhs-zite)*

Where is casualty?
Wo ist die Notaufnahme?
(voh ist dee <u>nort</u>-owf-nahm-me)

POLICE
POLIZEI

Call the police
Rufen Sie die Polizei *(roo-fen zee dee porl-lee-<u>tsy</u>)*

I have been robbed
Ich bin beraubt worden
(ikh been bay-<u>rowbt</u> vor-den)

My car has been stolen
Mein Auto ist gestohlen worden *(mine <u>ow</u>-to ist gay-<u>shtoh</u>-len vor-den)*

My car has been broken into
In mein Auto ist einge-brochen worden *(in mine <u>ow</u>-to ist ine-<u>gay</u>-bror-khen vor-den)*

I want to report a theft
Ich möchte einen Diebstahl melden *(ikh murkh-te inen <u>deeb</u>-shtahl <u>mel</u>-den)*

I have been attacked
Ich bin überfallen worden
(ikh bin oo-ber-<u>fahl</u>-len vor-den)

Where is the police station?
Wo ist die Polizeiwache? *(<u>voh</u> ist die por-lee-tsy-var-khe)*

EMERGENCIES
NOTFÄLLE

Call an ambulance
Rufen Sie einen Notwagen, Krankenwagen *(roof-fen zee inen <u>nort</u>-var-gen, <u>krahn</u>-ken-<u>var</u>-gen)*

There's been an accident
Es ist ein Unfall passiert *(ess ist ine <u>oon</u>-farl puss-seert)*

Someone is injured
Jemand ist verletzt *(<u>yay</u>-mond ist fer-<u>letst</u>)*

Hurry up!
Schnell! *(shnayll)*

Help!
Hilfe! *(<u>heel</u>-fe)*

Could you please help me?
Kannst du (fam) / Können Sie (pol) mir bitte helfen? *(carnst doo meer bitter <u>hel</u>-fen, cur-nen zee meer bitter <u>hel</u>-fen)*

My son/daughter is missing
Mein/e Sohn/Tochter ist verschwunden *(mine/r zorne/tokh-ter ist fer-<u>shvoon</u>-den)*

This is an emergency!
Es ist ein Notfall! *(ess ist ine <u>nort</u>-fahl)*

I need a report for my insurance
Ich brauche einen Bericht für meine Versicherung *(ikh <u>brow</u>-khe inen bay-<u>reekht</u> foor miner fer-<u>zee</u>-kher-roong)*

I want to phone my embassy
Ich möchte mit meiner Botschaft telefonieren *(ikh murkh'-te mit miner <u>bort</u>-shaft tel-le-phone-<u>near</u>-ren)*

I am lost
Ich habe mich verirrt *(ikh har-be meekh fer-<u>eert</u>)*

FIRE DEPARTMENT
FEUERWEHR

Fire!
Feuer! *(foyer)*

Look out!
Vorsicht! *(<u>for</u>-zeekht)*

Call the fire department please
Rufen Sie bitte die Feuerwehr *(<u>roof</u>-fen zee bitter dee <u>foyer</u>-vair)*

It's an electrical fire
Es ist ein Kabelbrand *(ess ist ine <u>car</u>-bell-brunt)*

The address is ...
Die Anschrift ist ... *(dee <u>arn</u>-shreeft ist ...)*

I need ...
Ich brauche ...
(ikh <u>brow</u>-khe ...)

◆ a fire extinguisher
◆ ein Feuerlöschgerät *(ine <u>foyer</u>-lursh-<u>gay</u>-rate)*

◆ medical assistance
◆ ärztliche Hilfe *(<u>ertst</u>-lee-kher <u>heel</u>-fe)*

THE HUMAN BODY
DER MENSCHLICHE KÖRPER

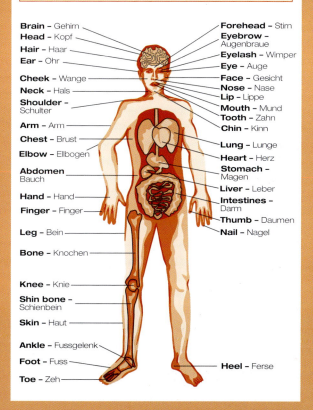

Brain – Gehirn
Head – Kopf
Hair – Haar
Ear – Ohr
Cheek – Wange
Neck – Hals
Shoulder – Schulter
Arm – Arm
Chest – Brust
Elbow – Ellbogen
Abdomen – Bauch
Hand – Hand
Finger – Finger
Leg – Bein
Bone – Knochen
Knee – Knie
Shin bone – Schienbein
Skin – Haut
Ankle – Fussgelenk
Foot – Fuss
Toe – Zeh

Forehead – Stirn
Eyebrow – Augenbraue
Eyelash – Wimper
Eye – Auge
Face – Gesicht
Nose – Nase
Lip – Lippe
Mouth – Mund
Tooth – Zahn
Chin – Kinn
Lung – Lunge
Heart – Herz
Stomach – Magen
Liver – Leber
Intestines – Darm
Thumb – Daumen
Nail – Nagel
Heel – Ferse

FORMS OF ADDRESS
ANREDE

There is quite a marked difference of approach to *Umgangsformen* (the way to behave in society) between the older and the younger generation. The former will usually adhere to the polite form of address – **Sie** – until such time as it is mutually agreed to progress to the familiar **du**. You should tread warily here, as you can put your counterpart in a spot by suggesting first-name terms (automatically implied when using the colloquial *du*). Young people are far more casual about this among themselves (especially in an informal set-up), but will generally adhere to the polite form when addressing older persons, or when they meet in a business environment.

Herr/Frau (*Fräulein* is very rarely used these days) implies that the person is an adult, either male or female, and that you are on polite terms. *Dr.* is an academic title and used as in English, but with the prefix *Herr/Frau*, since the person has earned the academic title in addition to his basic title: '*Frau Dr. Mayer, würden Sie bitte ...*' In the same way, a priest or cabinet minister would be addressed as *Herr Pastor/Minister*

(*Schmidt*) or *Frau Professor* (*Schmidt*). If *Pastor Schmidt* also holds a PhD it would depend on the circumstances, and your preference, how you address him verbally – the written address should read *Herr Pastor Dr. Alfred Schmidt.*

GREETINGS
GRUSSFORMELN

Greeting forms and shaking hands also tend to show a difference between the generations. Whereas it is correct to say *Guten Morgen, Guten Tag* or *Guten Abend,* young people will often greet each other with *Hallo* or *Hi* and not bother to shake hands. Generally, German people set a store by being greeted, preferably individually, or making individual eye contact. If in doubt rather greet once too often! Furthermore, there is a tendency to take things personally, so exercise some caution as far as witticisms and humorous comments are concerned.

THANK YOU
DANKEN

When invited to a meal in a private home it is appropriate to bring flowers for the hostess. (As you become more familiar, chocolates or wine can be substituted for the flowers). The 'Thank you' extended on leaving is deemed sufficient, and a follow-up phone call the next day is not expected. However, punctuality is important!

MANNERS
UMGANGSFORMEN

When you need to go to the bathroom make sure to ask for the *Toilette*, otherwise you might be shown the family bathroom with no toilet in sight (and your host is left wondering what you want to do in there). It is also important to close the lid of the toilet after use, and the door as well! To leave the door open (subjecting others to the flushing noises) is considered very ill mannered.

And speaking of noise, *Ruhe* is taken seriously in Germany. It used to be announced on the radio at 22:00 that you should turn down the volume of your set in order not to disturb your neighbours who might want to retire. So your hosts could admonish you to talk softly when you step outside at night. *Ruhe* is also the equivalent of not being disturbed, so don't phone before 08:00 or after 21:00, nor between 12:00 and 15:00, unless you know the person very well or have a sound reason.

Phone etiquette demands that the caller identifies himself/herself straight away – before stating his or her request. Germans usually say the family name when taking a call, much like a business.

Generally, Germans don't fall into line habitually (so there are no queues at bus stops), yet on other occasions they will fiercely demand their rightful turn, e.g. in a doctor's waiting room or at the counter of a post office or bank.

Another word of caution: Let German people bring up the subject of the War, if they feel like it. This subject matter tends to bring unexpected pitfalls or lengthy explanations.

HUMOUR
HUMOR

Germans like to make fun of others, but tend to be quite touchy themselves. They are also not keen to mix work and fun. In fact, there is an old saying: *Dienst ist Dienst, und Schnaps ist Schnaps* (duty is duty, and brandy is brandy), which implies that relaxing while on duty is not on! Germans do enjoy jokes, and their cabaret can be excellent, but you would have to be very fluent in the language and be up to date on both present and past issues to enjoy it.

DRIVING
AUTOFAHREN

Most Germans love their cars and they have strong opinions about the make and model they drive. Cars are serviced regularly and well cared for. There is an excellent road system and good signposting, but roads are busy, and on freeways the speed can be frightening! It may be advisable to stay in the slow lane. Watch out when changing lanes, as most Germans drive quite aggressively. Merging into a busy road can take a very long time. Conversely, you must be ready to accelerate the moment the traffic light changes, as drivers behind you expect this.

As in virtually all major European cities, parking is difficult to find in the city centres. In residential areas, observe the sign *Nur für Anlieger* (residents only) and stick to the speed limit.

Be prepared for long traffic jams on the *Autobahn* (at times stretching over several kilometres). When weather conditions are poor, you have to be highly alert, because Germany is notorious for pile-up traffic accidents.

As the public transport system is so efficient, it could save you trouble and possibly also work out cheaper than going by car.

New Year's Eve and New Year's Day

Silvester (31 December), *Neujahr* (1 January)
Exuberant parties and dances are held on 31 December – *Silvester* – so most people spend New Year's Day recovering.

Easter *Ostern*

(Good Friday, Easter Sunday and Easter Monday)
Special church services for all denominations, and homes are decorated with pretty craftwork. Of course there are Easter eggs, including painted hard-boiled eggs.

May Day, Labour Day

Maifeiertag (1 May)
In rural areas of the south maypoles are still quite popular, and special processions and church services are held in honour of the Virgin Mary.

Ascension Day

Christi Himmelfahrt (May)
This is also traditionally 'Father's Day', when men have a boisterous gentlemen's outing, called a *Herrenpartie*.

Pentecost

Pfingsten (May/June: Sunday and Monday)
Previously, new spring clothes were bought at this time.

Day of German Unity
Tag der Deutschen Einheit (3 October)
Celebrating East and West Germany's re-unification in 1990.

Christmas *Weihnachten* (24 December)
From the 1st Sunday of Advent private and public festivities mark this special season, leading up to the highlight, *Heiligabend* – Christmas Eve – when the family gathers for the *Bescherung* in the evening (exchange of gifts). Every family has its own particular timetable and menu, and many people go to church at this time, even if they are not observant otherwise.

REGIONAL HOLIDAYS
REGIONALE FEIERTAGE

Epiphany
Heilige Drei Könige (6 January)
In the Catholic regions children go around dressed up as the three Kings, singing songs, asking for a donation, and marking houses with chalk as a blessing.

Corpus Christi
Fronleichnam (usually June)
In the Catholic regions processions are held in the morning and sometimes there are open-air church services.

Assumption Day
Mariä Himmelfahrt
(15 August)
Special church services are held throughout the Catholic regions on Assumption Day.

Reformation Day
Reformationstag
(31 October)
This holiday marks the commemoration of Martin Luther's Reformation; special church services are held throughout the Protestant regions.

All Saints' Day
Allerheiligen (1 November)
Nowadays (in all the Catholic areas) there are still services held in the churchyard, or otherwise people visit the graves privately. Previously All Souls' Day (*Allerseelen*, 2 November) was also celebrated as a public holiday.

Day of Repentance and Prayer
Buss- und Bettag
(November)
This regional holiday is celebrated in Germany and Switzerland.

Immaculate Conception
Unbefleckte Empfängnis
(8 December)
Celebrated as a public holiday in Austria and also in the Catholic areas of Germany.

NATIONAL DAYS
NATIONALFEIERTAGE

Bundestag (1 August) Switzerland.

Tag der Deutschen Einheit (3 October) Germany.

Nationalfeiertag (26 October) **Austria.**

SPECIAL FESTIVALS
BESONDERE FESTE

Karneval/Fasching
Carnival is celebrated in the week before the beginning of Lent, mainly in Catholic southern Germany and especially in the Rhineland, but it has spread to other parts of the country as the (originally pagan) religious origins of the festival have become irrelevant.

Büttenabend
Evening entertainment, leading up to the masked ball on Shrove Tuesday, with humorous speakers, singing, etc.

Weiberfastnacht
Thursday before *Rosenmontag*, when women can let their hair down and 'attack' men, e.g. cut off their ties.

Rosenmontag
The Monday before Ash Wednesday, when decorated floats move through city streets.

These float parades mainly take place in Cologne, Düsseldorf, Bonn and Mainz.

Maskenball
Masked ball held on any evening of Carnival, but mainly on Shrove Tuesday, the highlight and end of the 'silly season' (*Narrenzeit*), which ends on Ash Wednesday, the onset of Lent.

Oktoberfest
Beer festival and fair in Munich, usually at the end of September.

Winzerfest
Wine festival, during and after the grape harvest in the wine-growing areas.

Christkindlmarkt
Christmas markets, which originated in southern Germany, but are now held countrywide. On sale are handmade tree decorations, candles, biscuits and traditional Christmas sweets.

Elferrat
The Council of Eleven, the 'fools' government', consisting of 11 men wearing suits and jesters' caps.

Strassenfeste
Eating, drinking, music (often dancing) and socializing, organized by the people of a neighbourhood. The festivities take place in the street.

ENGLISH → GERMAN

A

abbey Abtei f
abortion Abtreibung f
about (approximately)
  ungefähr
above oberhalb
abroad im Ausland
abscess Abszess m
absolutely genau
accelerator
  Gaspedal n
accent Akzent m
accept akzeptieren
accident Unfall m
accommodation
  Unterkunft f
account Rechnung f,
  das Konto n
accurate genau
ache Schmerz m
adapter Adapter
  (Zwischenstecker) m
adhesive tape
  Klebeband n
admission fee
  Eintrittspreis m
adult Erwachsene m
advance: in advance
  im Voraus
advert, advertisement
  Anzeige f
advise raten
aeroplane Flugzeug n
afraid, afraid of
  Angst haben vor
after nach
afternoon
  Nachmittag m

afterwards danach
again wieder
against gegen
age Alter n
ago: a week ago
  vor einer Woche
agree vereinbaren
agreement
  Vereinbarung f
air Luft f
air conditioning
  Klimaanlage f
air ticket Flugkarte f
airmail Luftpost f
airport Flughafen m
aisle Gang m
aisle seat Gangplatz m
all right in Ordnung
allow erlauben
almond Mandel f
almost fast
alone allein
already schon
also auch
although obwohl
altogether insgesamt
always immer
am: I am ich bin
a.m. (before noon)
  vormittags
amazing erstaunlich
amber gelb, Bernstein m
ambulance
  Krankenwagen m
among unter
amount Summe f,
  Betrag m, Menge f
anaesthetic Narkose f

ancient antik, alt
and und
angry zornig, verärgert
animal Tier n
ankle Knöchel m
anniversary
  Jahrestag m
annoy belästigen
annual jährlich
another ein weiteres,
  ein anderes, noch ein
answer Antwort f
ant Ameise f
antacid säurebindendes
  Mittel n
anybody irgendjemand
anything etwas, alles
apology Entschuldigung f
appendicitis
  Blinddarmentzündung f
appointment Termin m
apron Schürze f
are sind
area Gegend f
armchair Sessel m
arrange vereinbaren,
  regeln
arrest verhaften
arrival Ankunft f
art Kunst f
artist Künstler/in m/f
ask fragen
astonishing erstaunlich
at (place) am, bei
at (time) um
attack angreifen, Angriff
attic Dachboden,
  Speicher m

audience Publikum n
aunt Tante f
auto-teller
  Geldautomat m
autumn Herbst m
available erhältlich
avalanche Lawine f
avenue Allee f
average
  Durchschnitt m
avoid verhindern,
  meiden
awake wach
away weg
awful furchtbar

B
baby food
  Babynahrung f
back Rücken m
backache
  Rückenschmerzen f
backpack Rucksack m
bacon Speck m
bad schlecht
bag Tasche f
baggage Gepäck n
baggage claim
  Gepäckausgabe f
bait Köder m
bakery Bäckerei f
balcony Balkon m
ballpoint pen Kuli,
  Kugelschreiber m
Baltic Sea Östsee f
bandage Verband m
bar of chocolate
  Tafel Schokolade f

barber Herrenfrisör m
bark (n, tree) Rinde f
bark (vb, dog) bellen
barn Scheune f
barrel Fass n
basement Souterrain n, Erdgeschloss n
basket Korb m
bath Bad n
bathroom Badezimmer n
Bavaria Bayern
bay Bucht f
bay leaf Lorbeerblatt n
be sein
beach Strand m
bean Bohne f
beard Bart m
beautiful wunderschön
beauty salon Kosmetiksalon m
because weil
bed Bett n
bed & breakfast Übernachtung mit Frühstück
bee Biene f
beef Rindfleisch n
before vorher, bevor
beginner Anfänger m
behind hinten, hinter
Belgium Belgien
believe glauben
bell Glocke f
below unterhalb, unter
belt Gürtel m
bend (n) Kurve f
bend (vb) biegen, beugen
beside neben

better besser
beyond jenseits
bicycle Fahrrad n
big gross
bill Rechnung f
bin Mülleimer m
binoculars Fernglas n
bird Vogel m
birth Geburt f
birth certificate Geburtsurkunde f
birthday Geburtstag m
birthday card Geburtstagskarte f
birthday present Geburtstagsgeschenk n
biscuit Keks m
bit Stück n
bite Biss m
black schwarz
Black Forest Schwarzwald m
black ice Glatteis n
blackcurrant schwarze Johannisbeere f
blanket Decke f
bleach Bleichmittel n
bleed bluten
blind (adj) blind
blind (n) Rollo n, Jalousie f
blister Blase f
block of flats Wohnblock m
blocked verstopft
blood Blut n
blood pressure Blutdruck m

blouse Bluse f
blow-dry fönen
blue blau
blunt stumpf
blusher Rouge n
boar Wildschwein n
boarding card
  Bordkarte f
boat Schiff, Boot n
boat trip Bootsfahrt f
body Körper m
boil kochen
bone Knochen m
bonnet Motorhaube,
  Haube f
book (n) Buch n
book (vb) buchen
bookshop
  Buchhandlung f
boot (of car)
  Kofferraum m
boot (shoe) Stiefel m
border Grenze f
boring langweilig
born geboren
borrow borgen, leihen
both beide
bottle Flasche f
bottle opener
  Flaschenöffner m
bottom (at the) unten
bow tie Fliege f
bowl Schüssel f
box Karton m,
  Schachtel f
boy Junge m
boyfriend Freund m
bra BH m

bracelet Armband n
brake (n) Bremse f
brake (vb) bremsen
brake fluid
  Bremsflüssigkeit f
brake light Bremslicht n
branch (bank) Filiale f
branch (tree) Ast m
brand Marke f
brandy Weinbrand m
bread Brot n
break brechen
breakable zerbrechlich
breakdown (of car)
  Panne f
breakdown van
  Abschleppwagen m
breakfast Frühstück n
break-in Einbruch m
breast Brust f
breathe atmen
breeze Brise f
brewery Brauerei f
brick Ziegel m
bride Braut f
bridegroom
  Bräutigam m
bridge Brücke f
briefcase Aktentasche f
bright hell
bring bringen
Britain Grossbritannien
brochure Broschüre f
broken gebrochen
bronchitis Bronchitis f
brooch Brosche f
broom Besen m
brother Bruder m

ENGLISH → GERMAN

91

brother-in-law
  Schwager m
brown braun
bruise Bluterguss m
brush Bürste f, Pinsel m
Brussels Brüssel
bucket Eimer m
buffet car
  Speisewagen m
buggy Sportwagen m
build bauen
building Gebäude n
bulb (light) Glühbirne f
bulb (plant) Knolle f
bumper Stoßstange f
bunch Strauss m
bureau de change
  Wechselstube f
burglar Einbrecher m
burglary Einbruch m
burn (n) Verbrennung f
burn (vb) brennen,
  verbrennen
burst geplatzt, platzen
bus Bus m
bus stop Bushaltestelle f
bush Busch m
business Geschäft n
business trip
  Dienstreise f
busy beschäftigt
but aber
butcher Fleischer,
  Schlachter, Metzger m
butter Butter f
butterfly
  Schmetterling m
button Knopf m

buy kaufen
by (location) am
by (time) bis
bypass (road)
  Umgehung (Strasse) f

C
cab Taxi n, Taxe f
cabbage Kohl m
cabin Kabine f
cable car
  Drahtseilbahn f
cake Kuchen m
cake shop Konditorei f
calculator
  Taschenrechner m
calf Kalb n
call (n) Anruf m
call (vb) rufen
calm ruhig
camp zelten
camp site Zeltplatz,
  Campingplatz m
can (may) können
can (tin) Dose f
can opener
  Dosenöffner m
Canada Kanada
canal Kanal m
cancel stornieren
cancellation
  Stornierung f
cancer Krebs m
candle Kerze f
candy Süssigkeiten f
canoe Kanu n
cap (headgear) Mütze f
cap (lid) Deckel m

ENGLISH → GERMAN

capital (city)
Hauptstadt f
capital (money)
Kapital n
car Auto n
car ferry Autofähre f
car hire
Autovermietung f
car insurance
Kfz-Versicherung f
car key Autoschlüssel f
car parts
(Auto) Ersatzteile f
caravan Wohnwagen m
caravan site
Wohnwagenplatz m
carburettor
Vergaser m
card Karte f
cardboard Pappe f
cardigan Strickjacke f
careful vorsichtig
caretaker
Hausmeister m
carpenter Tischler m
carpet Teppich m
carriage Wagen m
carrier bag
Tragetasche f
carrot Karotte, Möhre f
carry tragen
carry-cot
Säuglingstragetasche f
carton Karton m,
Packung f
carwash
Autowaschanlage f
case Koffer m

cash (n) Bargeld n
cash (vb) einlösen
cash desk Kasse f
cash dispenser
Geldautomat m
cashier
Kassierer/in m/f
cassette Kassette f
castle Schloss n
casualty department
Unfallstation f
cat Katze f
catch fangen
cathedral Kathedrale f,
Dom m
Catholic katholisch,
Katholik/in m/f
cauliflower
Blumenkohl m
cave Höhle f
CD player CD-Spieler m
ceiling Zimmerdecke f
celery Sellerie m
cellar Keller m
cemetery Friedhof m
Centigrade Celsius
centimetre
Zentimeter m
central heating
Zentralheizung f
central locking
Zentralverriegelung f
centre Mitte f,
Zentrum n
century Jahrhundert n
certain sicher, gewiss
certainly gewiss, sicher

ENGLISH → GERMAN

certificate Bescheinigung f

chair Stuhl m

chair lift Sessellift m

chambermaid Zimmermädchen n

champagne Sekt m

change (n, money) Wechselgeld n

change (vb) ändern

change (vb, clothes) umziehen

change (vb, money) wechseln

change (vb, transport) umsteigen

changing room Umkleidekabine f

channel Kanal m

chapel Kapelle f

charcoal Holzkohle f

charge (vb, money) verlangen

charge card Kreditkarte f

charter flight Charterflug m

cheap billig

cheap rate Billigtarif m

cheaper billiger

check überprüfen, kontrollieren

check in sich anmelden, Check-in m

cheek Wange, Backe f

cheering jubeln

cheers! Prost! Zum Wohl!

cheese Käse m

chef Koch m, Köchin f

chemist Apotheker m, Apothekerin f

cheque Scheck m

cheque book Scheckbuch n

cheque card Scheckkarte f

cherry Kirsche f

chess Schach n

chest (anat) Brust f

chest (box) Kasten m

chest of drawers Kommode f

chestnut Kastanie f

chewing gum Kaugummi n/m

chicken Huhn, Hühnchen n

chicken pox Windpocken f

child Kind n

child car seat Kindersitz m

chimney Schornstein m

chin Kinn n

China China

china Porzellan n

chips Pommes frites fpl

chives Schnittlauch m

chocolate Schokolade f

chocolates Pralinen f

choir Chor m

choose wählen

chop hacken

Christian name Vorname m

Christmas Weihnachten

Christmas Eve
  Heiligabend **m**
church Kirche **f**
cider Apfelwein **m**
cigar Zigarre **f**
cigarette Zigarette **f**
cigarette lighter
  Feuerzeug **n**
cinema Kino **n**
circle Kreis **m**,
  Rang (theater) **m**
cistern Spülkasten **m**
citizen Bürger/in **m/f**
city Stadt **f**
city centre Stadt-
  zentrum **n**, Innenstadt **f**
class Klasse **f**
clean (adj) sauber
clean (vb) säubern
cleaning solution
  Reinigungslösung **f**
cleansing lotion
  Reinigungscreme **f**
clear klar
clever klug
client Kunde **m**,
  Kundin **f**
cliff Felsen **m**
climb klettern
cling film Frischhaltefolie **f**
clinic Klinik **f**
cloakroom
  Garderobe **f**
clock Uhr **f**
close schliessen
closed geschlossen
cloth Stoff, Lappen **m**

clothes Kleider **f**
clothes line
  Wäscheleine **f**
clothes peg
  Wäscheklammer **f**
cloud Wolke **f**
clutch Kupplung **f**
coach Bus **m**
coal Kohle **f**
coast Küste **f**
coastguard
  Küstenwache **f**
coat Mantel **m**
coat hanger
  Kleiderbügel **m**
cockroach Kakerlake,
  Küchenschabe **f**
cocoa Kakao **m**
coconut Kokosnuss **f**
cod Kabeljau **m**
code Kode, Vorwahl **f**
coffee Kaffee **m**
coil Spirale **f**
coin Münze **f**
Coke (Cola) Kola **f**
colander Sieb **n**
cold (adj) kalt
cold (n, med) Erkältung **f**
collapse
  zusammenbrechen
collar Kragen **m**
collar bone
  Schlüsselbein **n**
colleague Kollege **m**,
  Kollegin **f**
collect (fetch) abholen
collect (gather)
  sammeln

collect call R-Gespräch n
Cologne Köln
colour Farbe f
colour blind farbenblind
colour film Farbfilm m
comb Kamm m
come kommen, ankommen
come back zurückkommen
come in hereinkommen
comedy Komödie f
comfortable bequem
company Firma f
compartment Abteil n
compass Kompass m
complain beschweren
complaint Beschwerde f
completely völlig
composer Komponist/in m/f
compulsory obligatorisch
computer Computer m
concert Konzert n
concession Ermässigung f
concussion Gehirnerschütterung f
condition Zustand m
condom Kondom n/m
conference Konferenz f
confirm bestätigen
confirmation Bestätigung f

confused verwirrt
congratulations Glückwünsche pl
connecting flight Anschlussflug m
connection Verbindung f
conscious bei Bewusstsein
constipated verstopft
consulate Konsulat n
contact in Verbindung treten
contact lens Kontaktlinse f
continue weitermachen
contraceptive Verhütungsmittel n
contract Vertrag m
convenient günstig
cook (vb) kochen
cooker Herd m
cookie Plätzchen n
cooking utensil Küchengerät n
cool kühl
cool bag/box Kühltasche/box f
copy (n) Kopie f
copy (vb) kopieren
cork Korken m
corkscrew Korkenzieher m
corner Ecke f
correct (adj) richtig
corridor Flur m
cost (n) Kosten pl
cost (vb) kosten

cot Kinderbett n
cotton Baumwolle f
cotton wool Watte f
couch Sofa n
couchette
  Liegewagenplatz m
cough (n) Husten m
cough (vb) husten
cough mixture
  Hustensaft m
could (I) könnte (ich)
couldn't konnte nicht
counter Theke f
country Land n
countryside
  Landschaft f
couple, a couple
  Paar n, zwei
courier service
  Kurierdienst m
course (edu) Kurs m
course (meal) Gang m
cousin Kusine f, Vetter m
cover charge
  Gedeckkosten f
cow Kuh f
crab Krabbe f
craft Handwerk,
  Kunstgewerbe n
cramp Krampf m
crash Zusammenstoss,
  Unfall m
crash helmet
  Sturzhelm m
cream Sahne, Crème f,
  Rahm m
crèche Kinderkrippe f,
  Kinderhort m

credit card
  Kreditkarte f
crime Verbrechen n
crisps Chips f
crockery Geschirr n
cross Kreuz n
crossing Überfahrt f
crossroads Kreuzung f
crossword puzzle
  Kreuzworträtsel n
crowd Menge f
crowded voll, überfüllt
crown Krone f
cruise Kreuzfahrt f
crutches Krücken f
cry weinen
crystal Kristall m
cucumber Gurke f
cufflinks
  Manschettenknöpfe f
cup Tasse f
cupboard Schrank m
curly kraus
currency Währung f
current (elec) Strom m
current (water)
  Strömung f
curtain Vorhang m,
  Gardine f
cushion Kissen n
custard Vanillesosse f
custom Brauch m
customer Kunde m,
  Kundin f
customs Zoll m
cut (n) Schnitt m
cut (vb) schneiden
cutlery Besteck n

ENGLISH → GERMAN

cycle (time) Zyklus m
cycle (transport)
Fahrrad n
cycle track Radweg m
cyst Zyste f
cystitis
Blasenentzündung f
Czech Republic
Tschechische Republik,
Tschechien

D
daily täglich
damage (n) Schaden m
damage (vb)
beschädigen
damp feucht
dance (n) Tanz m
dance (vb) tanzen
danger Gefahr f
dangerous gefährlich
dark dunkel
date Datum n
date of birth
Geburtsdatum n
dates Datteln f
daughter Tochter f
daughter-in-law
Schwiegertochter f
dawn Morgen-
dämmerung f
day Tag m
dead tot
deaf taub
deal Geschäft n
dear (address) liebe/r
dear (expensive)
teuer

death Tod m
debts Schulden f
decaffeinated
koffeinfrei
December
Dezember m
decide entscheiden
decision
Entscheidung f
deck chair
Liegestuhl m
deduct abziehen
deep tief
definitely bestimmt
degree Grad m
delay (n) Verzögerung f
delay (vb) verzögern
deliberately absichtlich
delicious köstlich
deliver abliefern, liefern
delivery Ablieferung f
Denmark Dänemark
dental floss
Zahnseide f
dentist Zahnarzt m
dentures Gebiss n
depart abfahren
department Abteilung f
department store
Kaufhaus n
departure (by air)
Abflug m
departure (by road)
Abreise f
departure lounge
Abflughalle f
deposit Anzahlung f
describe beschreiben

description
  Beschreibung f
desk Schreibtisch m
dessert Nachtisch m
destination Reiseziel n
details Einzelheiten f
detergent
  Waschmittel n
detour Umweg m
develop entwickeln
diabetic
  Diabetiker/in m/f
dial wählen
dialling code Vorwahl f
dialling tone Wählton
  m, Freizeichen n,
diamond Diamant m
diaper Windel f
diarrhoea Durchfall m
diary (business)
  Terminkalender m
diary (personal)
  Tagebuch n
dice Würfel m
dictionary
  Wörterbuch n
die sterben
diesel Diesel
diet Diät f
difference
  Unterschied m
different verschieden,
  anders
difficult schwierig
dinghy Schlauchboot n
dining room
  Esszimmer n
dinner Abendessen n

direct direkt
direction Richtung f
directory (phone)
  Telefonbuch n
dirty schmutzig
disabled behindert
disappear
  verschwinden
disappointed
  enttäuscht
disaster Katastrophe f
disconnected
  abgeschnitten
discount Rabatt m
discover entdecken
disease Krankheit f
dish (crockery) Schale f
dish (meal) Gericht n
dishtowel
  Geschirrtuch n
dishwasher
  Geschirrspülmaschine f
disinfectant
  Desinfektionsmittel n
disk Diskette f
**disposable diapers/
  nappies**
  Papierwindeln fpl
distance Entfernung f
district Bezirk m
disturb stören
dive tauchen
diving board
  Sprungbrett n
divorced geschieden
DIY shop Baumarkt m
dizzy schwindelig
do machen

ENGLISH → GERMAN

doctor Arzt m, Ärztin f
document Dokument n
dog Hund m
doll Puppe f
domestic häuslich
door Tür f
doorbell Türglocke, Klingel f
doorman Portier m
double doppelt
double bed Doppelbett n
double room Doppelzimmer n
doughnut Berliner, Krapfen m
downhill abwärts
downstairs unten
dozen Dutzend n
drain Abfluss m
draught Durchzug m
draught beer Fassbier n
drawer Schublade f
drawing Zeichnung f
dreadful schrecklich
dress (n) Kleid n
dress (vb) anziehen
dressing (bandage) Verband m
dressing (salad) Salatsosse f
dressing gown Bademantel m, Morgenrock
drill Bohrer m
drink (n) Getränk n
drink (vb) trinken
drinking water Trinkwasser n

drive fahren
driver Fahrer/in m/f
driving licence Führerschein m
drop Tropfen m
drug Medikament n, Droge f
drunk betrunken
dry (adj) trocken
dry (vb) trocknen
dry cleaner's chemische Reinigung f
dryer Trockner m
duck Ente f
due fällig
dull stumpf, trübe
dummy Schnuller m
during während
dusk Abenddämmerung
dust Staub m
dustbin Mülltonne f
duster Staubtuch n, Staubwedel m
dustpan Schaufel f
Dutch holländisch
duty-free zollfrei
duvet Federbett n
duvet cover Bettbezug m
dye (n) Farbe f
dye (vb) färben
dynamo Lichtmaschine f

E
each jeder m, jede f, jedes n
eagle Adler m
ear Ohr n

earache
 Ohrenschmerzen f
earphones Kopfhörer f
earrings Ohrringe f
earth Erde f
earthquake Erdbeben n
east Osten m
Easter, Happy Easter!
 Ostern, Frohe Ostern!
Easter bunny
 Osterhase m
Easter egg Osterei n
easy leicht
eat essen
economy Wirtschaft f
economy class
 Touristenklasse f
edge Rand m, Kante f
eel Aal m
egg Ei n
either ... or
 entweder ... oder
elastic Gummi n/m
elbow Ellenbogen m
electric elektrisch
electrician Elektriker m
electricity Elektrizität f,
 Strom m
elevator Aufzug m
embassy Botschaft f
emergency Notfall m
emergency exit
 Notausgang m
empty leer
end (n) Ende n
end (vb) beenden
**engaged (telephone,
 toilet)** besetzt

**engaged (to be
 married)** verlobt
engine Motor m
engineer
 Ingenieur/in m/f
England England
English englisch
Englishman/woman
 Engländer/in m/f
enjoy geniessen
enlargement
 Vergrösserung f
enough genug
enquiry Nachfrage f
enquiry desk
 Auskunft f
enter eintreten
Enter! Herein!
entrance Eingang m
entrance fee
 Eintrittsgebühr f,
 Eintrittspreis m
envelope Umschlag m
epileptic
 Epileptiker/in m/f
equipment
 Ausrüstung f
error Fehler m
escalator Rolltreppe f
escape entkommen
especially besonders
essential wesentlich
estate agent
 Immobilienmakler m
Estonia Estland
Europe Europa
European europäisch
even sogar

ENGLISH → GERMAN

ENGLISH → GERMAN

evening Abend m
eventually schliesslich
every, everyone jeder
  m, jede f, jedes n
everything alles
everywhere überall
exactly genau
examination (med)
  Untersuchung
examination (test)
  Prüfung f
example, for example
  Beispiel n, zum Beispiel
excellent ausgezeichnet
except ausser
excess luggage
  Übergewicht n
exchange Austausch,
  Umtausch m
exciting aufregend
exclude ausschliessen
excursion Ausflug m
excuse me please
  entschuldigen Sie bitte
exhaust pipe
  Auspuffrohr n
exhausted erschöpft
exhibition Ausstellung f
exit Ausgang m
expect erwarten
expenses Spesen f
expensive teuer
experienced erfahren
expire verfallen
explain erklären
explosion Explosion f
export Ausfuhr f,
  Export m

exposure (film)
  Belichtung f
express (mail)
  Express, Eilbrief m
express (train)
  Schnellzug m
extension lead
  Verlängerungskabel n
extra zusätzlich
extraordinary
  aussergewöhnlich
eye Auge n
eye drops
  Augentropfen f
eye make-up remover
  Augen-Make-up-
  Entferner m
eye shadow
  Lidschatten m
eyeglasses Brille f

F
face Gesicht n
factory Fabrik f
faint ohnmächtig werden
fair (fête) Messe,
  Kirmes f
fair (hair colour) blond
fair (just) gerecht
fairly ziemlich
fake Fälschung f
fall (n) Herbst m
fall (vb) fallen
false falsch
family Familie f
famous berühmt
fan Fächer, Ventilator,
  Fan m

fan belt Keilriemen m
far weit
fare Fahrpreis m
farm Bauernhof m
farmer Bauer m, Bäuerin f
farmhouse Bauernhaus n
fashionable modisch
fast schnell
fasten befestigen
fasten seatbelt sich anschnallen
fat dick
father Vater m
father-in-law Schwiegervater m
fatty fett
fault Fehler m
faulty defekt
favourite Lieblings-
fax Fax n
February Februar m
feed füttern
feel fühlen
feet Füsse f
female weiblich
fence Zaun m
fender Stoßstange f
ferry Fähre f
festival Fest n
fetch holen
fever Fieber n
few, a few wenige, ein paar
fiancée Verlobte/r f/m
field Feld n
fight (vb) kämpfen

file (folder) Datei f, Ordner m, Akte f
file (tool) Feile f
fill, fill in, fill up füllen, ausfüllen, voll tanken
fillet Filet n
filling (sandwich) Belag m
filling (tooth) Füllung f
film (n) Film m
film processing Filmentwicklung f
filter Filter m
filthy dreckig, schmutzig
find finden
fine (adj) schön
fine (n) Geldstrafe f
finger Finger m
finish (n) Ende n
finish (vb) beenden
fire Feuer n
fire brigade Feuerwehr f
fire exit Notausgang m
fire extinguisher Feuerlöscher m
first, at first Erste/r f/m, zuerst
first aid Erste Hilfe f
first-aid kit Verbandkasten m
first class Erste Klasse
first floor Erster Stock
first name Vorname m
fish (n) Fisch m
fish (vb) fischen
fishing permit Angelschein m
fishing rod Angelrute f

ENGLISH → GERMAN

103

fishmonger's
Fischhandlung f
fit (n) Anfall m
fit (vb) passen
fitting room
Anproberaum m
fix reparieren
fizzy sprudelnd
flag Flagge, Fahne f
flannel Waschlappen m
flash Blitzlicht n
flashlight Taschenlampe f
flask Thermosflasche f
flat (adj) flach
flat (n) Wohnung f
flat battery leere
Batterie f
flat tyre Reifenpanne f
flavour Geschmack m
flaw Mangel, Fehler m
flea Floh m
flight Flug m
flip flops Latschen f
flippers
Schwimmflossen f
flood Flut f
floor Boden m, Etage f
floorcloth
Scheuerlappen m
florist Blumen-
händler/in m/f
flour Mehl n
flower Blume f
flu Grippe f
fluent fliessend
fly (n) Fliege f
fly (vb) fliegen
fog Nebel m

follow folgen
food Essen n
food poisoning
Speisevergiftung f
food shop
Lebensmittelgeschäft n
foot Fuss m
football Fussball m
football match
Fussballspiel n
footpath Fussweg m
for für
forbidden verboten
forehead Stirn f
foreign ausländisch
foreigner
Ausländer/in m/f
forest Wald m
forget vergessen
fork Gabel, Gabelung f
form Formular n
formal formell
fortnight zwei Wochen
fortress Festung f
fortunately
glücklicherweise
fountain Quelle f
four-wheel drive
Allradantrieb m
fox Fuchs m
fracture
Knochenbruch m
frame Rahmen m
France Frankreich
free frei, gratis
freelance freiberuflich
freeway Autobahn f
freezer Gefriertruhe f

French französisch
French fries Pommes frites f
Frenchman/woman Franzose/Französin m/f
frequent häufig
fresh frisch
Friday Freitag m
fridge Kühlschrank m
fried gebraten
friend Freund/in m/f
friendly freundlich
frog Frosch m
from von, aus, ab
front Vorderseite f
frost Frost m
frozen gefroren
fruit Frucht f, Obst n
fruit juice Fruchtsaft m
fry braten
frying pan Bratpfanne f
fuel Benzin n, Sprit m
fuel gauge Tankanzeige f
full voll
full board Vollpension f
fun Spass m
funeral Beerdigung f
funicular Seilbahn f
funny komisch
fur Pelz m
fur coat Pelzmantel m
furnished möbliert
furniture Möbel f
further weiter
fuse Sicherung f
fuse box Sicherungskasten m
future Zukunft f

G
gallery Galerie f
gallon Gallone f
game (animal) Wild n
game (play) Spiel n
garage Garage, Tankstelle f
garden Garten m
garlic Knoblauch m
gas Gas n, Benzin (USA)
gas cooker Gasherd m
gas cylinder Gasflasche f
gate Tor n
gay homosexuell
gear Gang m
gear lever Schaltknüppel m
gearbox Getriebe n
general allgemein
generous grosszügig
Geneva Genf
gents' (toilet) Herrentoilette f
genuine echt
German deutsch, Deutsche m/f
German measles Röteln f
get (obtain) bekommen
get on, get off einsteigen, aussteigen
get to hinkommen
gift Geschenk n
girl Mädchen n
girlfriend Freundin f

ENGLISH → GERMAN

105

ENGLISH → GERMAN

give geben
give back zurückgeben
glacier Gletscher m
glad froh
glass Glas n
glasses (spectacles) Brille f
gloves Handschuhe f
glue Leim, Klebstoff m
go (by car) fahren
go (on foot) gehen
go away weggehen
go back zurückgehen
goat Ziege f
God Gott m
goggles (snow) Schneebrille f
goggles (water) Tauchbrille f
gold Gold n
golf club Golfschläger m
golf course Golfplatz m
good gut
good afternoon, good day Guten Tag
good evening Guten Abend
Good Friday Karfreitag
good morning Guten Morgen
good night Gute Nacht
goodbye Auf Wiedersehen
goose Gans f
Gothic gotisch
government Regierung f
gradually allmählich
gram Gramm n

grammar Grammatik f
grand grossartig
granddaughter Enkelin f
grandfather Grossvater m
grandmother Grossmutter f
grandparents Grosseltern
grandson Enkel m
grapes Weintrauben f
grass Gras n
grated geraspelt, gerieben
grateful dankbar
gravy Sauce, Sosse f
greasy fettig
great grossartig
Great Britain Grossbritannien
Greece Griechenland
Greek griechisch
green grün
greengrocer Gemüsehändler m
greeting Gruss m
grey grau
grilled gegrillt
ground Boden m
ground floor Erdgeschoss n
group Gruppe f
guarantee (n) Garantie f
guarantee (vb) garantieren
guard Wache f
guest Gast m

guesthouse Pension f
guide Fremden-
führer/in m/f
guidebook
Reiseführer m
guided tour
Rundgang m, Rund-
fahrt f, mit Führung
guitar Gitarre f
gun Gewehr n
gym Fitness-Studio n

H

hail Hagel m
hair Haare pl
hairbrush Haarbürste f
haircut Haarschnitt m
hairdresser Friseur m
hairdryer Fön m
half (adj, adv) halb
half (n) Hälfte f
hall Diele f
ham Schinken m
hamburger
Hamburger m
hammer Hammer m
hand Hand f
hand luggage
Handgepäck n
handbag Handtasche f
handbrake
Handbremse f
handicapped behindert
handkerchief
Taschentuch n
handle Griff m
handmade
handgearbeitet

handsome
gutaussehend
hang up (phone)
auflegen
hanger Kleiderbügel m
hang-gliding
Drachenfliegen n
hangover Kater m
happen geschehen
happy glücklich
harbour Hafen m
hard hart
hard disk Festplatte f
hardly kaum
hardware shop
Eisenwarenhandlung f
hare Hase m
harvest Ernte f
hat Hut m
have haben
hay fever
Heuschnupfen m
hazelnuts Haselnüsse f
he er
head Kopf m
headache
Kopfschmerzen f
headlight
Scheinwerfer m
headphones Kopfhörer m
health food shop
Bioladen m
healthy gesund
hear hören
hearing aid Hörgerät n
heart Herz n
heart attack
Herzanfall m

ENGLISH → GERMAN

heartburn
 Sodbrennen n
heat (n) Hitze f
heat (vb) heizen
heater Ofen m
heating Heizung f
heavy schwer
heel (foot) Ferse f
heel (shoe) Absatz m
height Höhe f
helicopter
 Hubschrauber m
helmet Schutzhelm m
Help! Hilfe!
help (vb) helfen
hem Saum m
her ihr/sie
herbal tea
 Kräutertee m
herbs Kräuter f
here hier
hernia Bruch m
hide (vb) verstecken
high hoch
high blood pressure
 hoher Blutdruck
high chair
 Kinderstuhl m
high tide Flut f
him ihm/ihn
hip Hüfte f
hip replacement
 künstliches Hüftgelenk
hire (n) Vermietung f
hire (vb) mieten
hire car Mietauto n
his sein/seines
historic historisch

history Geschichte f
hit schlagen
hitchhike trampen
hold (contain) enthalten
hold (keep) halten
hole Loch n
holiday Feiertag m
holidays Urlaub m
holy heilig
home Zuhause n
homesickness
 Heimweh n
honest ehrlich
honey Honig m
honeymoon
 Flitterwochen f
hood Haube, Kapuze f
hope (n) Hoffnung f
hope (vb) hoffen
hopefully hoffentlich
horn Hupe f
horse Pferd n
horse racing
 Pferderennen n
horse riding Reiten n
hose pipe Garten-
 schlauch m
hospital Krankenhaus n
hospitality
 Gastfreundschaft f
hostel Wohnheim n
hot heiss
hot spring
 Thermalquelle f
hot-water bottle
 Wärmflasche f
hour Stunde f
hourly stündlich

house Haus n
house wine Hauswein m
housework Hausarbeit f
hovercraft Luftkissen-
fahrzeug n
how wie
How are you? Wie
geht es Ihnen?
How do you do?
Guten Tag!
how many wieviel/e
How much is it? Was/
Wieviel kostet es?
humid feucht, schwül
humour Humor m
Hungarian ungarisch
Hungary Ungarn
hungry hungrig
hunt jagen
hunting permit
Jagderlaubnis f,
Jagdschein m
hurry (n) Eile f
hurry (vb) eilen
hurt verletzt
hurts schmerzt
husband Ehemann m
hydrofoil Tragflächenboot n
hypodermic needle
Spritze f

I
I ich
ice Eis n
ice cream Eis n
ice rink Schlittschuhbahn f

ice skates Schlitt-
schuhe f
iced coffee Eiskaffee m
idea Idee f
identity card
Ausweis m
if wenn
ignition Zündung f
ignition key
Zündschlüssel m
ill krank
illness Krankheit f
immediately sofort
important wichtig
impossible unmöglich
improve verbessern
in in, im
inch Zoll m
included inbegriffen
inconvenient ungünstig
incredible unglaublich
Indian indisch,
Inder/in m/f
indicator Blinker m
indigestion
Magenverstimmung f
indoor pool
Hallenbad n
indoors drinnen
infection Infektion f
infectious ansteckend
inflammation
Entzündung f
informal zwanglos
information Auskunft f
ingredients Zutaten f
injection Spritze f
injured verletzt

ENGLISH → GERMAN

ENGLISH → GERMAN

injury Verletzung **f**
ink Tinte **f**
in-laws Schwieger-
eltern **f**
inn Gasthaus **n**
inner tube Schlauch
(Reifen) **m**
insect Insekt **n**
insect bite
Insektenstich **m**
insect repellent
Insektenschutzmittel **n**
inside innen
insist darauf bestehen
insomnia Schlaflosigkeit **f**
instant coffee
Pulverkaffee **m**
instead statt dessen
insulin Insulin **n**
insurance
Versicherung **f**
intelligent intelligent
interesting interessant
international
international
interpreter
Dolmetscher/in **m/f**
intersection Kreuzung **f**
interval Pause **f**
into in
introduce vorstellen
invitation Einladung **f**
invite einladen
invoice Rechnung **f**
Ireland Irland
Irish irisch
Irishman/woman
Ire **m**, Irin **f**

iron (n, appliance)
Bügeleisen **n**
iron (n, metal) Eisen **n**
iron (vb) bügeln
ironing board
Bügelbrett **n**
ironmonger's
Eisenwarenhandlung **f**
is ist
island Insel **f**
it es
Italian italienisch,
Italiener/in **m/f**
Italy Italien
itch jucken

J
jack Wagenheber **m**
jacket Jacke **f**
jam Konfitüre **f**
jammed verklemmt
January Januar **m**
jar Glas **n**
jaundice Gelbsucht **f**
jaw Kiefer **m**
jealous eifersüchtig
jellyfish Qualle **f**
jersey Strickjacke **f**
Jew Jude **m**, Jüdin **f**
jeweller Juwelier **m**
jewellery Schmuck **m**
Jewish jüdisch
job Anstellung **f**
jog joggen
join beitreten
joint Gelenk **n**
joke (n) Witz **m**
joke (vb) scherzen

journey Reise f
joy Freude f
jug Krug m
judge Richter m
juice Saft m
July Juli m
jump (n) Sprung m
jump (vb) springen
jump leads
  Starthilfekabel n
jumper Pullover m
junction Kreuzung f
June Juni m
just (fair) gerecht
just (only) nur

K
keep behalten
Keep the change! Es
  stimmt so!
kettle Wasserkessel m
key Schlüssel m
key ring
  Schlüsselhalter m
kick (n) Tritt m
kick (vb) kicken, treten
kidney Niere f
kill töten
kilo, kilogram Kilo,
  Kilogramm n
kilometre Kilometer m
kind nett
king König m
kiosk Kiosk m
kiss Kuss m
kitchen Küche f
kitchenette
  Kochnische f

knee Knie n
knickers Schlüpfer m,
  Höschen n
knife Messer m
knit stricken
knitting needle
  Stricknadel f
knitwear Strickware f
knock (on door) klopfen
knock against stossen
knock over umstossen
**knocked down (by a
  car)** angefahren
**knocked down (de-
  molished)** abgerissen
know wissen, kennen

L
label Etikett n
lace Spitze f
ladder Leiter f
ladies (toilet)
  Damentoilette f
ladies' wear
  Damenkleidung f
lady Dame f
lager helles Bier
lake See m
Lake Constance
  Bodensee m
Lake Lucerne
  Vierwaldstätter See m
lamb Lamm n
lamp Lampe f
land (n) Land n
land (vb) landen
landlady Vermieterin f
landlord Vermieter m

ENGLISH → GERMAN

landslide Erdrutsch m
lane (motorway) Fahrbahn f
lane (road) Gasse f
language Sprache f
language course Sprachkurs m
large gross
last letzte f, letzter m, letztes n
last night gestern Abend
late spät
later später
Latvia Lettland
laugh lachen
launderette, laundromat Waschsalon m
laundry (clothes) Wäsche f
laundry (place) Wäscherei f
lavatory Toilette f
law Gesetz n
lawyer Rechtsanwalt m
laxative Abführmittel n
lazy faul
lead (elec) Kabel n
lead (metal) Blei n
lead (vb) führen
lead-free bleifrei
leaf Blatt n
leaflet Prospekt m
leak (n) Leck n
leak (vb) lecken
learn lernen
lease (n) Mietvertrag m
leather Leder n
leave verlassen

leave (by car, bus) wegfahren
leave (on foot) weggehen
leave behind hinterlassen
leek Lauch m
left links
left-handed Linkshänder/in m/f
leg Bein n
lemon Zitrone f
lemonade Limonade f
lend leihen
lens Linse f
lentils Linsen fpl
lesbian lesbisch
less weniger
lesson Unterrichtsstunde f
let lassen, vermieten
let off absetzen
letter Brief m
letterbox Briefkasten m
lettuce Kopfsalat m
level crossing Bahnübergang m
lever Hebel m
library Bibliothek, Leihbücherei f
licence Genehmigung f, Führerschein m
lid Deckel m
lie (n) Lüge f
lie (vb) liegen
lie down hinlegen
life Leben n
life belt Rettungsring m

life guard Rettungs-
schwimmer **m**
life insurance
Lebensversicherung **f**
life jacket Schwimm-
weste **f**
lift (elevator) Aufzug **m**
lift (n) Mitfahrgelegenheit **f**
lift (vb) heben
light (adj) leicht, hell
light (n, cigarette)
Feuer **n**
light (n, elec) Licht **n**
light bulb Glühbirne **f**
lightning Blitz **m**
like mögen, gefallen
lime Limone **f**
line (on paper) Linie **f**
line (phone) Leitung **f**
linen Leinen **n**,
Weisswäsche **f**
lingerie Unterwäsche **f**
lion Löwe **m**
lipstick Lippenstift **m**
liqueur Likör **m**
list (n) Liste **f**
list (vb) auflisten
listen zuhören
Lithuania Litauen
litre Liter **m**
litter Abfall **m**
little klein, bisschen
live leben, wohnen
lively lebhaft
liver Leber **f**
living room
Wohnzimmer **n**
loaf Brotlaib **m**

lobby Foyer **n**
lobster Hummer **m**
local örtlich
lock (n) Schloss **n**
lock (vb) zuschliessen
lock in einschliessen
lock out ausschliessen
locker Schliessfach **n**
lollipop Lutscher **m**
long lang/lange
long-distance call
Ferngespräch **n**
look after sich
kümmern um
look at anschauen
look for suchen
look forward to sich
freuen auf
loose lose
lorry Last(kraft)wagen **m**,
LKW
lose verlieren
lost verloren, verlaufen
lost property
Fundbüro **n**
lot viel
loud laut
lounge Wohnzimmer **n**,
Warteraum **m**
love (n) Liebe **f**
love (vb) lieben
lovely schön
low niedrig
low fat fettarm
low tide Ebbe **t**
luck, good luck!
Glück **n**, viel Glück!
lucky glücklich

ENGLISH → GERMAN

ENGLISH → GERMAN

luggage Gepäck n
luggage rack
Gepäckablage f
luggage tag
Gepäckanhänger m
luggage trolley
Gepäckwagen,
Kofferkuli m
lump Schwellung f
lunch Mittagessen n
lung Lunge f
Luxembourg
Luxemburg
luxury Luxus m

M
machine Maschine f
mad verrückt, irr
made gemacht,
hergestellt
magazine Zeitschrift f
maggot Made f
magnet Magnet m
magnifying glass
Vergrösserungsglas n
maid Zimmermädchen n
maiden name
Mädchenname m
mail Post f
main Haupt-
main course
Hauptgang m
main post office
Hauptpostamt n
main road Haupt-
strasse f
mains switch
Hauptschalter m

make (n) Marke f
make (vb) machen
male männlich
man Mann m
manager Geschäfts-
führer/in m/f
man-made fibre
Kunstfaser f
manual (n)
Gebrauchsanweisung,
Handschaltung f
many viele
map Landkarte f, Stadtplan m, Strassenkarte f
marble Marmor m
March März m
market Markt m
marmalade
Marmelade f
(Orangenmarmelade)
married verheiratet
marsh Sumpf m
mascara
Wimperntusche f
mashed potatoes
Kartoffelpüree n
Mass (rel) Messe f
mast Mast m
match Wettspiel n
matches (for lighting)
Streichhölzer pl
matches (games)
Wettspiele pl
material Stoff m,
Material n
matter Sache f
**matter: it doesn't
matter** macht nichts!

matter: what's the matter was ist los?

mattress Matratze f

May Mai m

may darf

maybe vielleicht

mayonnaise Mayonnaise f

me mir/mich

meal Mahlzeit f

mean (intend) bedeuten

mean (nasty) gemein

measles Masern f

measure messen

meat Fleisch n

mechanic Mechaniker m

medical insurance Krankenversicherung f

medicine Medizin f

medieval mittelalterlich

Mediterranean Sea Mittelmeer n

medium mittel

medium dry (wine) halbtrocken (Wein)

medium rare (meat) halbdurch (Fleisch)

medium sized mittelgross

meet treffen

meeting Besprechung f

melon Melone f

melt schmelzen

men Männer pl

mend reparieren, flicken

meningitis Hirnhautentzündung f

menswear Herrenbekleidung f

mention erwähnen

menu Speisekarte f

meringue Baiser n

message Nachricht f

metal Metall n

meter Zähler m

metre Meter m

metro U-Bahn f

microwave Mikrowelle f

midday Mittag m

middle Mitte f

midnight Mitternacht f

might könnte

migraine Migräne f

mile Meile f

milk Milch f

minced meat Hackfleisch n

mind (n) Geist m

mineral water Mineralwasser n

minister (church) Pfarrer m

minister (politics) Minister m

mint Pfefferminz m

minute Minute f

mirror Spiegel m

Miss Fräulein n

miss verpassen

missing verschwunden

mist Nebel m

mistake Fehler, Irrtum m

misunderstanding Missverständnis n

ENGLISH → GERMAN

ENGLISH → GERMAN

mix mischen
mix-up Verwechslung f
mobile phone
Mobiltelefon, Handy n
moisturizer
Feuchtigkeitscreme f
moment Moment m
monastery Kloster n
Monday Montag m
money Geld n
money belt Gürtel-
tasche f
money order Post-
anweisung f
month Monat m
monthly monatlich
monument Denkmal n
moon Mond m
mooring Anlegestelle f
more mehr
morning, this morning
Morgen m, heute
Morgen
mosque Moschee f
mosquito Moskito m,
Stechmücke f
most meiste/n
mostly meistens
moth Motte f
mother Mutter f
mother-in-law
Schwiegermutter f
motor Motor m
motorbike Motorrad n
motorboat Motor-
boot n
motorway Autobahn f
mountain Berg m

mountain rescue
Bergwacht f
mountaineering
Bergsteigen n
mouse Maus f
moustache
Schnurrbart m
mouth Mund m
mouth ulcer Mund-
geschwür n
mouthwash Mund-
wasser n
move bewegen
move house verziehen,
umzienen
Mr Herr
Mrs/Ms Frau
much viel
mud Schlamm m
mug Trinkbecher m
mugged überfallen
mumps Mumps m
Munich München
muscle Muskel f
museum Museum n
mushroom Pilz m
music Musik f
musician
Musiker/in m/f
Muslim muslimisch,
Muslime m, Muslimin f
mussels Muscheln fpl
must muss
mustard Senf m
mutton Hammel-
fleisch n
my mein
myself selbst

N

nail Nagel m
nail brush Nagel-
bürste f
nail file Nagelfeile f
nail polish/varnish
Nagellack n
nail polish remover
Nagellackentferner m
nail scissors
Nagelschere f
name Name m
nanny Kinder-
mädchen n
napkin Serviette f
nappy Windel f
narrow eng
nasty gemein
national national
nationality Staats-
angehörigkeit f
natural natürlich
nature Natur f
nature reserve Natur-
schutzgebiet n
nausea Übelkeit f
navy Marine f
navy blue marineblau
near nahe
nearby in der Nähe
nearly beinahe, fast
necessary notwendig
neck Genick n, Hals m
necklace Halskette f
need brauche
needle Nadel f
negative (adj) negativ
negative (n) Negativ n

neighbour Nachbar m
neither ... nor
weder ... noch
nephew Neffe m
nervous breakdown
Nervenzusammen-
bruch m
nest Nest n
net Netz n
Netherlands
Niederlande
never nie, niemals
new neu
**New Year, Happy
New Year!** Neujahr n,
Frohes Neues Jahr!
New Year's Eve
Silvester
**New Zealand, New
Zealander** Neusee-
land, Neuseeländer/in
news Nachrichten fpl
news stand Zeitungs-
kiosk m
newspaper Zeitung f
next nächste/r
nice schön, gut
niece Nichte f
night, last night
Nacht f, gestern Nacht
nightdress Nacht-
hemd n
no nein, kein
nobody niemand
noise Lärm m
noisy laut
non-alcoholic
alkoholfrei

117

non-smoking Nichtraucher
none keine/r
noon Mittag m
north Norden m
Northern Ireland Nordirland
North Sea Nordsee f
Norway Norwegen
Norwegian norwegisch
nose Nase f
not nicht
note (n, money) Geldschein m
note (n, paper) Notiz f
note (vb) aufmerken
notebook/paper Notizbuch/papier n
nothing nichts
nothing else sonst nichts
notice board Anschlagbrett n
novel Roman m
November November m
now jetzt
nudist beach FKK-Strand m
number Nummer f
number plate Nummernschild n
Nuremberg Nürnberg
nurse, male nurse Krankenpflegerin f, Krankenpfleger m
nursery Kinderstube f
nursery school Vorschule f

nursery slope Anfängerhügel m
nut Nuss f
nut (for bolt) Schraubenmutter f

O
oak Eiche f
oar Ruder n
oats Hafer m
obtain erhalten
occasionally gelegentlich
occupation Beruf m
occupied (toilet) besetzt
ocean Ozean m
October Oktober m
odd eigenartig
odd number ungerade Zahl
of von
off (food) verdorben
off (switch) aus
office Büro m
often oft
oil Öl n
ointment Salbe f
OK in Ordnung
old alt
old-age pensioner Rentner/in m/f
old-fashioned altmodisch
olive Olive f
olive oil Olivenöl n
omelette Omelett n
on (date) am

on (position) auf
on (switch) an
once einmal
one eins, eine/r
one-way street
  Einbahnstrasse f
onion Zwiebel f
only nur
open (adj) offen,
  geöffnet
open (vb) aufmachen
open ticket
  unbeschränkter
  Fahr/Flugschein
opening times
  Öffnungszeiten f
opera Oper f
operation Operation f
operator (phone)
  Vermittlung f
opposite gegenüber,
  entgegengesetzt
optician Optiker m
or oder
orange Orange,
  Apfelsine f
orange juice Orangen-
  saft m
orchestra Orchester n
order (n) Bestellung f
order (vb) bestellen
organic (vegetables)
  Bio(gemüse) n
other andere
otherwise sonst
our unser/e
out aus, nicht da
out of order kaputt

outdoors draussen
outside ausserhalb,
  draussen
oven herd m
ovenproof feuerfest
over über, vorüber
over here hier
over there dort
overcharge zuviel
  berechnen
overcoat Überzieher m
overdone verkocht
overheat überhitzen
overnight über Nacht
overtake überholen
owe schulden
owl Eule f
owner Eigentümer m,
  Eigentümerin f

P
pacemaker
  (Herz)schrittmacher m
pack packen
package Packung f
package holiday
  Pauschalreise f
packet Paket n
padlock Vorhänge-
  schloss n
page (n) Seite f
page (vb) ausrufen
paid bezahlt
pail Eimer m
pain Schmerz m
painful schmerzhaft
painkiller Schmerz-
  mittel n

ENGLISH → GERMAN

paint (n) Farbe f
paint (vb) malen
painting Gemälde n
pair Paar n
palace Palast m
pale blass
pan Pfanne f
pancake Pfann-
kuchen m
panties Unterhöschen f
pants Hosen f
pantyhose Strumpf-
hosen f
paper Papier n
paper napkins Papier-
servietten f
parcel Paket n
pardon? Wie bitte?
parents Eltern f
parents-in-law
Schwiegereltern f
park (n) Park m
park (vb) parken
parking disc
Parkscheibe f
parking meter Parkuhr f
parking ticket Straf-
zettel, Parkschein m
part Teil m
partner Partner/in m/f
party (celebration)
Party, Fete f
party (group) Gruppe f
party (political) Partei f
pass (n) Passierschein m
pass (vb) vorbeigehen
pass control
Passkontrolle f

passenger Passagier,
Fahrgast m
passport Reisepass m
past Vergangenheit f
pastry Teig m,
Gebäck n
path Weg m
patient Patient m
pattern Muster n
pavement
Bürgersteig m
pay bezahlen
payment Bezahlung f
payphone
Münztelefon n,
Münzfernsprecher m
pea Erbse f
peach Pfirsich m
peak Gipfel m
peak rate Höchstrate f
peanut Erdnuss f
pear Birne f
pearl Perle f
peculiar eigenartig
pedal Pedal n
pedestrian
Fussgänger m
pedestrian crossing
Fussgängerübergang m
peel schälen
peg (clothes) Wäsche-
klammer f
peg (tent) Zelthering m
pen Schreiber m
pencil Bleistift m
penfriend Brief-
freund/in m/f
peninsula Halbinsel f

people Leute,
Menschen **pl**
pepper Pfeffer **m**,
Paprikaschote **f**
per pro
perfect perfekt
performance
Vorstellung **f**
perfume Parfüm **n**
perhaps vielleicht
period Periode, Zeit **f**
perm Dauerwelle **f**
permit Genehmigung **f**
person Person **f**
pet Haustier **n**
petrol Benzin **n**
petrol can Benzin-
kanister **m**
petrol station
Tankstelle **f**
pharmacy Apotheke **f**
phone (n) Telefon **n**
phone (vb)
telefonieren
phone book
Telefonbuch **n**
phone booth
Telefonzelle **f**
phone call Anruf **m**
phone card
Telefonkarte **f**
phone number
Telefonnummer **f**
**photo, to take a
photo** Foto **n**, ein
Foto machen
photocopy Fotokopie,
Ablichtung **f**

phrase book
Sprachführer **m**
piano Klavier **n**
pickpocket
Taschendieb **m**
picnic Picknick **n**
picture Bild **n**
picture frame
Bilderrahmen **m**
pie Pastete **f**, ein
gedeckter Kuchen **m**
piece Stück, Teil **n**
pig Schwein **n**
pill Tablette, Pille **f**
pillow Kopfkissen **n**
pillowcase
(Kopf)kissenbezug **m**
pilot Pilot **m**
pin Stecknadel **f**
pineapple Ananas **f**
pink rosa
pipe Pfeife **f**
pity, it's a pity schade,
das ist schade
place (n) Platz **m**
place (vb) platzieren
plain einfach
plait Zopf **m**
plane Flugzeug **n**
plant Pflanze **f**
plaster Pflaster **n**,
Gips **m**
plastic Plastik **n**
plastic bag
Plastiktüte **f**
plate Teller **m**
platform Bahnsteig **m**
play (n) Aufführung **f**

ENGLISH → GERMAN

play (vb) spielen
playground
  Spielplatz m
please bitte
pleased, Pleased to meet you! erfreut, Sehr erfreut!
plenty viel
pliers Zange f
plug (elec) Stecker m
plug (sink) Stöpsel m
plum Pflaume f
plumber Klempner m
p.m. nachmittags
poached pochiert
pocket Tasche f
point Punkt m
points (car)
  Kontakte mpl
poison Gift n
poisonous giftig
Poland Polen
police Polizei f
police station
  Polizciwache f
policeman/woman
  Polizist/in m/f
Polish polnisch
polish (n) Politur f
polish (vb) polieren
polite höflich
polluted verschmutzt
pool Schwimmbecken n
poor (impecunious)
  arm
poor (quality) schlecht
poppy Mohn m
popular beliebt

population
  Bevölkerung f
pork Schweinefleisch n
port (harbour)
  Hafen m
port (wine)
  Portwein m
porter Gepäckträger m
portion Portion f
portrait Portrait n
Portugal Portugal
Portuguese portugiesisch, Portugiese m, Portugiesin f
posh vornehm
possible möglich
post (n) Post f
post (vb) absenden
post box Briefkasten m
post office Postamt n
postage Porto n
postage stamp
  Briefmarke f
postal code
  Postleitzahl f
postcard Postkarte f
poster Plakat n
postman/woman
  Briefträger/in m/f
postpone verschieben
potato Kartoffel f
pothole Schlagloch n
pottery Töpferwaren fpl
pound Pfund n
pour giessen
powder Puder m
powdered milk
  Trockenmilch f

power cut Stromausfall m
practice Praxis f
practise üben
pram Kinderwagen m
prawn Garnele f
pray beten
prefer vorziehen
pregnant schwanger
prescription Rezept n
present (adj) anwesend
present (n) Geschenk n
pressure Druck m
pretty hübsch
price Preis m
priest Priester m
prime minister
Premierminister,
Kanzler m
print (n) Abzug m
print (vb) drucken
printed matter Drucksache f
prison Gefängnis n
private privat
prize Preis m
probably wahrscheinlich
problem Problem n
programme, program
Programm n
prohibited verboten
promise (n)
Versprechen n
promise (vb)
versprechen
pronounce
aussprechen
properly richtig

Protestant evangelisch,
Protestant/in m/f
public öffentlich
public holiday
gesetzlicher Feiertag n
pudding Nachtisch m
pull ziehen
pullover Pullover m
pump Pumpe f
puncture Reifenpanne f
puppet show
Marionettentheater n
purple violett
purse Geldbörse f
push stossen, schieben
pushchair Kinderkarre f
put hinstellen
put ... up unterbringen
pyjamas Schlafanzug m

Q

quality Qualität f
quantity Quantität,
Menge f
quarantine
Quarantäne f
quarrel streiten
quarter Viertel n
quay Kai m
queen Königin f
question Frage f
queue (n)
Warteschlange f
queue (vb) anstehen
quickly schnell
quiet leise, Ruhe f
quilt Bettdecke f
quite ziemlich

ENGLISH → GERMAN

ENGLISH → GERMAN

R

rabbit Kaninchen n
rabies Tollwut f
race (people) Rasse f
race (sport) Rennen n
race course
Rennbahn f
racket Schläger m
radiator (car)
Kühler m
radiator (room) Heiz-
körper m, Heizung f
radio Radio n,
Rundfunk m
radish Radieschen n
rag Lappen m
railway Eisenbahn f
railway station
Bahnhof m
rain (n) Regen m
rain (vb) regnen
raincoat Regen-
mantel m
raisin Rosine f
rake Harke f
rape (n) Vergewaltigung f
rape (vb) vergewaltigen
rare (seldom) selten
rare (steak) blutig
rash Ausschlag m
raspberry Himbeere f
rat Ratte f
rate (of exchange)
Wechselkurs m
raw roh
razor Rasierapparat m
razor blades
Rasierklingen fpl

read lesen
ready bereit, fertig
real echt
realize erkennen
really wirklich
rearview mirror
Rückspiegel m
reasonable vernünftig
receipt Quittung f
receiver (phone)
Hörer m
receiver (radio)
Empfänger m
recently kürzlich
reception Empfang m
receptionist
Empfangschef m,
Empfangsdame f
recharge aufladen
recipe (Koch)Rezept n
recognize erkennen
recommend empfehlen
record (n, legal)
Unterlage f
record (n, music)
Schallplatte f
red rot
red wine Rotwein m
redcurrants rote
Johannisbeeren fpl
reduce reduzieren
reduction
Ermässigung f
refund Rückerstattung f
refuse (n) Müll f
refuse (vb) ablehnen
region Gebiet n
register (n) Register n

register (vb) eintragen, anmelden
registered mail per Einschreiben
registration form Anmeldeformular n
registration number Kennzeichen n, Autonummer f
relative, relation Verwandte/r f/m
remain bleiben
remember erinnern
rent (n) Miete f
rent (vb) mieten
repair (n) Reparatur f
repair (vb) reparieren
repeat wiederholen
reply (n) Antwort f
reply (vb) antworten
report (n) Bericht m
report (vb) berichten
request (n) Bitte f
request (vb) erbitten
require benötigen
rescue (n) Rettung f
rescue (vb) retten
reservation Buchung, Reservierung f
reserve reservieren, buchen
resident Bewohner/in m/f
resort Urlaubsgebiet n
rest (relax) Ruhe f
rest (remainder) Rest m
retired pensioniert

return (give back) zurückgeben
return (in vehicle) zurückfahren
return (on foot) zurückgehen
return ticket Rückfahrkarte f
reverse rückwärts fahren
reverse-charge call R-Gespräch n
reverse gear Rückwärtsgang m
revolting ekelhaft
rheumatism Rheumatismus m
Rhine Rhein m
rib Rippe f
ribbon Band n
rice Reis m
rich (food) reichhaltig
rich (wealthy) reich
ride reiten
ridiculous lächerlich
right (correct) richtig
right (direction) rechts
right-hand drive Rechtssteuerung f
ring (n) Ring m
ring (vb) klingeln
ring road Umgehungsstrasse f
rip-off Wucher m
ripe reif
river Fluss m
road Strasse f
road accident Verkehrsunglück n

ENGLISH → GERMAN

ENGLISH → GERMAN

road map Strassen-
karte f
road sign Verkehrs-
schild n
roadworks Strassen-
arbeiten fpl
rock Felsen m
roll Brötchen n
roof Dach n
roof-rack Dach-
gepäckträger m
room Zimmer n
rope Seil n
rose Rose f
rotten verfault
rough rauh
round (adj) rund
round (n) Runde f
roundabout Kreis-
verkehr m
row (n) Reihe f
row (vb) rudern
royal königlich
rubber Gummi m
rubbish Abfall m
Rubbish! Quatsch!
rubella Röteln f
rudder Ruder n
rug Teppich m
ruin Ruine f
ruler Herrscher m
ruler Lineal n
rum Rum m
run rennen
rush eilen
rusty rostig
rye bread Roggen-
brot n

S
sad traurig
saddle Sattel m
safe (adj) sicher
safe (n) Safe m
safety belt
Sicherheitsgurt m
safety pin
Sicherheitsnadel f
sail (n) Segel n
sail (vb) segeln
sailing Segeln n
salad Salat m
salad dressing
Salatsauce f
sale Ausverkauf,
Verkauf m
sales representative
Vertreter/in m/f
salesperson
Verkäufer/in m/f
salmon Lachs m
salt Salz n
same dasselbe
sand Sand m
sandals Sandalen fpl
sandwich ein belegtes
Brot n
sanitary pads Damen-
binden fpl
Saturday Samstag,
Sonnabend m
sauce Sauce, Sosse f
saucer Untertasse f
sausage Wurst f
save (money) sparen
save (rescue) retten
savoury pikant

say sagen
scales Waage f
scarf Schal m
scenery Landschaft f
school Schule f
scissors Schere f
Scot Schotte m, Schottin f
Scotland Schottland
Scottish schottisch
scrambled eggs Rühreier pl
scratch (n) Kratzer m
scratch (vb) kratzen
screen Bildschirm m
screw Schraube f
screwdriver Schraubenzieher m
scrubbing brush Scheuerbürste f
scuba diving Sporttauchen n
sea See f, Meer n
seagull Möwe f
seasickness Seekrankheit f
seaside Küste f
season Jahreszeit f
season ticket Zeitkarte f
seasoning Gewürz n
seat Sitz, Platz m
seat belt Sicherheitsgurt m
seaweed Seetang m
secluded abgelegen
second (adj) zweite/r/s
second (n) Sekunde f

second class Zweiter Klasse
second hand gebraucht
secretary Sekretär/in m/f
security guard Wache f
see sehen
self-catering selbstversorgend
self-employed freiberuflich tätig
self-service Selbstbedienung f
sell verkaufen
sell-by date Haltbarkeitsdatum n
send senden
senior citizens Senioren pl
sentence (grammar) Satz m
sentence (law) Verurteilung f
separate getrennt
September September m
septic vereitert
septic tank Klärgrube f
serious schlimm, ernst
service Dienst m
service charge Bedienungsgeld n
set menu Tageskarte f
several mehrere, einige
sew nähen

127

sex (gender)
Geschlecht n
sex (intercourse)
Sex m
shade Schatten m
shake schütteln
shallow seicht
shame Schande f
shampoo and set
Waschen und Legen
share teilen
sharp scharf
shave rasieren
she sie
sheep Schaf n, Schafe pl
sheet Laken n
shelf Regal n
shellfish Krustentier f
sheltered geschützt
shine scheinen, glänzen
shingle Dachziegel m
shingles Gürtelrose f
ship Schiff n
shirt Hemd n
shock absorber
Stossdämpfer m
shoe Schuh m
shoe laces
Schnürsenkel f
shop Geschäft n
shop assistant
Verkäufer/in m/f
shop window
Schaufenster n
shopping centre
Einkaufszentrum n
shore Ufer n
short kurz

short-cut Abkürzung f
short-sighted
kurzsichtig
shorts Shorts f
should sollte
shoulder Schulter f
shout (n) Schrei m
shout (vb) schreien
show (n) Aufführung f
show (vb) zeigen
shower (n) Dusche f
shower (vb) duschen
shrimps Krabben fpl
shrink einlaufen
shut geschlossen,
schliessen, zu
shutter Fensterladen m
shy schüchtern
sick krank
side Seite f
side dish Beilage f
sidewalk Bürgersteig m
sieve Sieb n
sight Sehenswürdigkeit f
sightseeing Sehens-
würdigkeiten besichtigen
sign unterschreiben,
Schild n
signal Signal n
signature Unterschrift f
signpost Wegweiser m
silence Stille f
silk Seide f
silly albern
silver Silber n
similar ähnlich
simple einfach
sing singen

singer Sänger/in m/f
single ledig, Einzel-,
  einfach (one-way ticket)
single bed Einzelbett n
single room Einzel-
  zimmer n
sink Abwaschbecken n
sister Schwester f
sister-in-law
  Schwägerin f
sit setzen, sitzen
size Grösse f
skate (n) Schlittschuh,
  Rollschuh m
skate (vb) Schlittschuh
  laufen
skating rink Eisbahn f
ski (n) Ski m
ski (vb) Ski fahren/laufen
ski boot Skistiefel m
ski jump Sprung-
  schanze f
ski slope (Ski) Piste f
skin Haut f
skirt Rock m
sky Himmel m
sledge Schlitten m
sleep schlafen
sleeper, sleeping car
  Schlafwagen m
sleeping bag Schlaf-
  sack m
sleeping pill Schlaf-
  tablette f
sleepy müde, schläfrig
slice Scheibe f
slide (photo) Dia n
slip (n) Unterrock m

slip (vb) rutschen
slippers Hausschuhe pl
slippery rutschig
Slovak Slowake m,
  Slowakin f
Slovak Republic
  Slowakische Republik,
  Slowakei
slow, slowly langsam
small klein
smell (n) Geruch m
smell (vb) riechen
smile (vb) lächeln
smoke (n) Rauch m
smoke (vb) rauchen
smoked salmon
  geräucherter Lachs m
snack Imbiss m
snake Schlange f
sneeze niesen
snore schnarchen
snorkel (n)
  Schnorchel m
snorkel (vb) schnorcheln
snow, it is snowing
  Schnee m, es schneit
soaking solution
  Einweichlösung f
soap Seife f
soap powder Wasch-
  pulver n
sober nüchtern
socket Steckdose f
socks Socken pl
soda Sodawasser n
soft weich
soft drink ein alkoholfreies Getränk n

ENGLISH → GERMAN

ENGLISH → GERMAN

sole (fish) Seezunge f
sole (shoe) Sohle f
soluble löslich
some einige
someone, somebody jemand
something etwas
sometimes manchmal
somewhere irgendwo
son Sohn m
son-in-law Schwiegersohn m
song Lied n
soon bald
sore, it's sore schmerzhaft, es tut weh
sore throat Halsschmerzen f
Sorry! Entschuldigung!
sort Sorte f
soup Suppe f
sour sauer
south Süden m
South Africa Südafrika
South African südafrikanisch, Südafrikaner/in m/f
souvenir Andenken n
spa Kurort m
spade Spaten m
Spain Spanien
Spaniard Spanier/in m/f
Spanish spanisch
spanner Schraubenschlüssel m
spare part Ersatzteil n
spare tyre/wheel Ersatzreifen m

spark plug Zündkerze f
sparkling sprudelnd
speak sprechen
speciality Spezialität f
spectacles Brille f
speed Geschwindigkeit f
speed limit Geschwindigkeitsbegrenzung f
speedometer Tachometer m
spell buchstabieren
spend ausgeben
spice Gewürz n
spider Spinne f
spill verschütten
spin-dryer Schleuder f
spinach Spinat m
spine Rückgrat n
spirits Spirituosen fpl
splinter Splitter m
spoil verderben
spoke (of wheel) Speiche f
sponge Schwamm m
spoon Löffel m
sprain (n) Verstauchung f
sprain (vb) verstauchen
spring (n, metal) Feder f
spring (n, season) Frühling m
spring (vb) springen
square Rechteck n, Platz m
stadium Stadion n
stain Fleck m

stairs Treppe f
stale alt, abgestanden, altbacken
stamp Briefmarke f
staple zusammenheften
star Stern m
start anfangen
starter (car) Anlasser m
starter (food) Vorspeise f
station Bahnhof m
stationer's Schreibwarenhandlung f
statue Statue f
stay bleiben, wohnen
steal stehlen
steam Dampf m
steep steil
steer lenken
steering wheel Lenkrad n
step Stufe f
stepfather Stiefvater m
stepmother Stiefmutter f
stew Eintopf m
stick (vb) kleben
sticking plaster Heftpflaster n
still (quiet) still
still (yet) noch
sting (n) Stachel m
sting (vb) stechen
stitch nähen, Stich m
stock Brühe, Bouillon f
stocking Strumpf m
stolen gestohlen

stomach Magen m
stomachache Magenschmerzen f
stone Stein m
stop (n) Stoppschild n
stop (vb) anhalten
stopover Zwischenstation f
store Laden m, Geschäft n
storey Stockwerk n
storm Sturm m
straight gerade
straight on geradeaus
straightaway sofort
strange seltsam
stranger Fremde/r f/m
strap Band n
straw Stroh n
strawberry Erdbeere f
stream Bach m
street Strasse f
street map Strassenkarte f
strike Streik m
string Schnur f
striped gestreift
stroke (clock) Schlag m
stroke (med) Schlaganfall m
strong stark
stuck geklemmt, festgesteckt
student Student/in m/f
student discount Studentenermässigung f
stuffed (taxidermy) ausgestopft

stuffed (turkey) gefüllt
stupid dumm
subtitle Untertitel m
suburb Vorort m
subway U-Bahn f
suddenly plötzlich
suede Wildleder n
sugar Zucker m
sugar-free zuckerfrei
suit (female) Kostüm n
suit (male) Anzug m
suitcase Koffer m
summer Sommer m
summit Gipfel m
sun Sonne f
sun block Sonnen-
  schutzcreme f
sunburn
  Sonnenbrand m
Sunday Sonntag m
sunglasses Sonnen-
  brille f
sunny sonnig
sunrise Sonnen-
  aufgang m
sunroof Sonnendach n
sunset Sonnen-
  untergang m
sunshade Sonnen-
  schirm m
sunshine Sonnen-
  schein m
sunstroke Sonnen-
  stich m
suntan Sonnenbräune f
suntan lotion Sonnen-
  creme f
supper Abendessen n

supplement Beilage f
sure gewiss
surfboard Surfbrett n
**surgery (doctor's
  rooms)** Arztpraxis f
surgery (procedure)
  Operation f, Eingriff m
surname Nachname m
surrounded umgeben
suspension (car)
  Federung f
**suspension (from
  school)** Ausschluss m
swallow schlucken
swear (an oath)
  schwören
swear (curse) fluchen
swear word Fluchwort n
sweat (n) Schweiss m
sweat (vb) schwitzen
sweater Pullover m
Swede Schwede m,
  Schwedin f
Sweden Schweden
Swedish schwedisch
sweet (adj) süss
sweet (n) Süssigkeit f
swell schwellen
swelling Schwellung f
swim schwimmen
swimming costume
  Badeanzug m
swing Schaukel f
Swiss Schweizer/in m/f
Swiss-German
  Schweizerdeutsch
switch Schalter m
switch off ausschalten

switch on einschalten
Switzerland Schweiz f
swollen geschwollen
synagogue Synagoge f

T

table Tisch m
table tennis Tischtennis
table wine Tafelwein m
tablecloth Tischtuch n
tablespoon Esslöffel m
tailor Schneider m
take nehmen
take-away food Essen
  zum Mitnehmen
talcum powder
  Körperpuder n
talk sprechen
tall lang, hoch
tampon Tampon m
tan (n) Bräune f
tan (vb) bräunen
tangerine Mandarine f
tank Tank m
tape Kassette f
tape measure
  Massband n
tape recorder
  Kassettenrekorder m
taste kosten, schmecken
tax Steuer f
taxi Taxi n, Taxe f
taxi driver Taxifahrer m
taxi rank Taxistand m
tea Tee m
tea bag Teebeutel m
teach unterrichten
teacher Lehrer/in m/f

team Team n,
  Mannschaft (sport) n
teapot Teekanne f
tear (n) Riss m
tear (vb) reissen
teaspoon Teelöffel m
teeth Zähne pl
telephone (n) Telefon n
telephone (vb)
  telefonieren
telephone call Anruf m
television Fernseher m
tell sagen, erzählen
temperature
  Temperatur f, Fieber n
temple (face) Schläfe f
temple (rel) Tempel m
temporary vorüber-
  gehend, provisorisch
tendon Sehne f
tennis Tennis n
tennis court
  Tennisplatz m
tennis racket
  Tennisschläger m
tent Zelt n
tent peg Zelthering m
terminal (airport)
  Abfertigungshalle f
terminal (bus)
  Endstation f
terminal (computer)
  Terminal n
thank danken
that das, jene/r/s
the der m, die f, das n,
  die pl
theatre Theater n

theft Diebstahl m
there da, dort
thermometer Thermometer n
they sie
thick dick
thief Dieb m
thigh Schenkel m
thin dünn
thing Ding n
think denken
third-party insurance Haftpflichtversicherung f
thirsty durstig
this dies
this diese/r/s
thorn Dorn m
those jene
thousand tausend
thread Faden m
throat Kehle f, Hals m
throat lozenges Halspastillen pl
through durch
throw werfen
thumb Daumen m
thunder Donner m
thunderstorm Gewitter n
Thursday Donnerstag m
ticket Karte, Fahrkarte f
ticket: single, return Fahrkarte: einfach, Rückfahrkarte f
ticket collector Schaffner/in m/f
ticket office Fahrkartenschalter m

tide, low tide, high tide Gezeiten pl, Ebbe f, Flut f
tie Schlips m, Krawatte f
tight eng
tights Strumpfhosen pl
till (cash register) Kasse f
till (until) bis
time, What's the time? Zeit f, Wie spät ist es? Wieviel Uhr ist es?
timetable Fahrplan m
tin Dose f
tin opener Dosenöffner m
tinfoil Alufolie f
tiny winzig
tip Trinkgeld n
tired müde
tissue Papiertaschentuch n
to nach, zu/r/m
today heute
toe Zeh m
together zusammen
toilet Toilette f
toll, toll road Zoll m, Zollstrasse f
tomato Tomate f
tomato juice Tomatensaft m
tomorrow morgen
tomorrow morning/afternoon/evening morgen früh/nachmittag/abend
tongue Zunge f

tonight heute Abend
tonsillitis Mandel-
entzündung **f**
too (also) auch
too (degree) zu
tool Werkzeug **n**
toolkit Werkzeug-
kasten **m**
tooth Zahn **m**
toothache Zahn-
schmerzen **pl**
toothbrush Zahn-
bürste **f**
toothpick Zahn-
stocher **m**
top oben
top floor oberste
Stockwerk **n**
topless oben ohne
torch Taschenlampe **f**
torn zerrissen
total Endsumme **f**
tough zäh
tour Reise, Führung **f**
tour guide
Reiseleiter/in **m/f**
tour operator
Reiseveranstalter/in **m/f**
tow abschleppen
towel Handtuch **n**
tower Turm **m**
town Stadt **f**
town hall Rathaus **n**
toy Spielzeug **n**
tracksuit Trainings-
anzug **m**
traffic Verkehr **m**
traffic jam Stau **m**

traffic light Ampel **f**
trailer Anhänger **m**
train Zug **m**
tram Strassenbahn **f**
tranquillizer
Beruhigungsmittel **n**
translate übersetzen
translation Über-
setzung **f**
translator Über-
setzer/in **m/f**
trash Abfall **m**
travel reisen
travel agency Reise-
büro **n**
travel documents
Reisepapiere **pl**
travel sickness
Reisekrankheit **f**
traveller's cheque
Reisescheck **m**
tray Tablett **n**
tree Baum **m**
trolley Einkaufswagen,
Gepäckwagen **m**
trouble Schwierigkeit **f**
trousers Hose **f**
trout Forelle **f**
truck Laster,
Lastwagen **m**
true wahr
trunk Koffer **m**
try, try on versuchen,
anprobieren
tuna Thunfisch **m**
tunnel Tunnel **m**
Turk, Turkish Türke **m**,
Türkin **f**, türkisch

ENGLISH → GERMAN

ENGLISH → GERMAN

turkey Truthahn m,
Pute f
Turkey Türkei f
turn, turn around
drehen, umdrehen
turn off abbiegen,
ausschalten
turquoise türkis
tweezers Pinzette f
twice zweimal
twin beds zwei
Einzelbetten pl
twins Zwillinge
type tippen
typical typisch
tyre Reifen m
tyre pressure
Reifendruck m

U

ugly hässlich
ulcer Geschwür n
umbrella Schirm m
uncle Onkel m
uncomfortable
unbequem
unconscious
bewusstlos
under unter
underdone (meat)
nicht gar, nicht durch
underground (adj)
Untergrund-
**underground (n,
metro)** U-Bahn f
underpants Unter-
hose f
understand verstehen

underwear Unter-
wäsche pl
unemployed arbeitslos
United Kingdom
Vereinigtes Königreich
United States
Vereinigte Staaten
university Universität f
unleaded petrol
bleifreies Benzin n
unlimited unbeschränkt
unlock aufschliessen
unpack auspacken
unscrew aufschrauben
until bis
unusual ungewöhnlich
up, to get up auf,
aufstehen
upside down verkehrt
herum
upstairs oben
urgent dringend
us uns
use benutzen
useful nützlich
usual, usually üblich,
gewöhnlich

V

vacancy (B&B, hotel)
freies Zimmer n
vacancy (job) Freistelle f
vacation Urlaub m,
Semesterferien f
vaccination
Schutzimpfung f
vacuum cleaner
Staubsauger m

valid gültig
valley Tal n
valuable wertvoll
value Wert m
valve Ventil n
van Lieferwagen m
vanilla Vanille f
VAT (value added tax)
  MWS (Mehrwertsteuer) f
veal Kalbfleisch n
vegetables Gemüse n
vegetarian
  Vegetarier/in m/f
vehicle Fahrzeug n
vein Vene, Ader f
vending machine
  Automat m
venereal disease
  Geschlechtskrankheit f
very sehr
vest Unterhemd n
vet (veterinarian)
  Tierarzt m, Tierärztin f
via über
Vienna Wien
view Aussicht f
village Dorf n
vinegar Essig m
vineyard Weinberg m
violet Veilchen n
virus Virus m
visa Visum n
visit (n) Besuch m
visit (vb) besuchen
visiting hours
  Besuchszeit f
visitor Besucher/in m/f
voice Stimme f

volcano Vulkan m
voltage Strom-
  spannung f
vomit erbrechen
voucher Gutschein m

W
wage Lohn m
waist Taille f
waistcoat Weste f
wait warten
waiter/waitress
  Kellner/in m/f
waiting room
  Warteraum m
wake up aufwachen
wake-up call
  Weckruf m
Wales Wales
walk (n) Spaziergang m
walk (vb) gehen
wall Wand, Mauer f
wallet Brieftasche f
walnut Walnuss f
want möchten, wollen
war Krieg m
ward (hospital) Station f
wardrobe Kleider-
  schrank m
warehouse Lagerhalle f
warm warm
wash waschen
washbasin Wasch-
  becken n
washing powder
  Waschpulver n
washing-up liquid
  Spülmittel n

ENGLISH → GERMAN

ENGLISH → GERMAN

wasp Wespe f
waste vergeuden
waste bin Abfall-
eimer m
watch (n) Armbanduhr f
watch (vb) zuschauen
watch strap
Uhrenarmband n
water Wasser n
water skiing Wasserski
laufen
watermelon Wasser-
melone f
waterproof wasser-
dicht
wave Welle f
way, this way Weg m,
hier entlang
we wir
weak schwach
wear (clothing) tragen
weather Wetter n
weather forecast
Wettervorhersage f
web Netz n
wedding Hochzeit f
wedding present
Hochzeitsgeschenk n
wedding ring
Ehering m
Wednesday
Mittwoch m
week last/this/next
Woche f, letzte/diese/
nächste
weekday Wochentag m
weekend Wochen-
ende n

weekly wöchentlich
weigh wiegen
weight Gewicht n
weird seltsam
welcome willkommen
well gut
Welsh Waliser/in m/f,
walisisch
were waren
west Westen m
wet nass
wetsuit Tauchanzug m
what? was?
wheel Rad n
wheel clamp
Parkkralle f
wheelchair Rollstuhl m
when? wann?
where? wo?
which? welche/r/s?
while während
whipped cream
Schlagsahne f,
Schlagrahm m
white weiss
who? wer?
whole vollständig, ganz
wholemeal bread
Vollkornbrot n
whose? wessen?
why? warum?
wide weit
widow, widower
Witwe f, Witwer m
wife Ehefrau f
wig Perücke f
win gewinnen
wind Wind m

window Fenster n
window seat
Fensterplatz m
windscreen
Windschutzscheibe f
windscreen wiper
Scheibenwischer m
windy windig
wine Wein m
wine list Weinkarte f
winter Winter m
wire Draht m
wish (n) Wunsch m
wish (vb) wünschen
with mit
without ohne
witness Zeuge m,
Zeugin f
wolf Wolf m
woman Frau f
wood (forest) Wald m
wood (timber) Holz n
wool Wolle f
word Wort n
work (n) Arbeit f
work (vb, job) arbeiten
work (vb, machine)
funktionieren
world Welt f
worried besorgt
worse schlimmer
worth wert
wrap up einwickeln
wrapping paper
Geschenkpapier n,
Einwickelpapier n
wrinkles Falten pl
wrist Handgelenk n

wristwatch
Armbanduhr f
write schreiben
writing paper
Briefpapier n
**wrong, what is
wrong?** falsch, was
ist los?

X
X-ray Röntgen-
aufnahme f

Y
yacht Jacht f
year Jahr n
yellow gelb
Yellow Pages Gelbe
Seiten pl
yes ja
yesterday gestern
yolk Eigelb n
you (formal) Sie
you (familiar) du
young jung
your dein
youth hostel
Jugendherberge f

Z
zero null
zipper, zip fastener
Reissverschluss m
zone Zone f
zoo Zoo m

ENGLISH → GERMAN

GERMAN → ENGLISH

A

Aal m eel
ab from
abbiegen turn off
Abend m evening
Abendessen n dinner, supper
aber but
abfahren depart (by car, bus)
Abfall m litter, trash
Abfalleimer m waste bin, rubbish can
Abflug m departure (airport)
Abflughalle f departure lounge
Abfluss m drain
Abführmittel n laxative
abgelegen secluded
abgeschnitten disconnected
abgestanden stale
abholen collect
Abkürzung f short-cut
ablehnen refuse (vb)
Ablichtung f photocopy
Ablieferung f delivery
Abreise f departure
Absatz m heel (shoe)
abschleppen tow
Abschleppwagen m breakdown van
absenden post (vb)
absetzen let off
absichtlich deliberately
Abszess m abscess

Abtei f abbey
Abteil n compartment
Abteilung f department
Abtreibung f abortion
abwärts downhill
Abwaschbecken n (kitchen) sink
abziehen deduct
Abzug m print (photo)
Adapter m adapter
Adler m eagle
ähnlich similar
Aktentasche f briefcase
Akzent m accent
akzeptieren accept
albern silly
alkoholfrei non-alcoholic
alkoholfreies Getränk n soft drink
Allee f avenue
allein alone
alles everything, anything
allgemein general
allmählich gradually
Allradantrieb m four-wheel drive
alt ancient, old, stale
altbacken stale (bread)
Alter n age
altmodisch old-fashioned
Alufolie f tinfoil
am at, by (location), on (date)
Ameise f ant
Ampel f traffic light

140

an on (switch)
Ananas f pineapple
Andenken n souvenir
andere other
ändern change (vb)
anders different
Anfall m fit (n)
Anfang m start (n)
anfangen start (vb)
Anfänger m beginner
Anfängerhügel m
  nursery slope
angefahren knock
  down
Angelrute f fishing rod
Angelschein m fishing
  permit
angreifen attack (vb)
Angriff m attack (n)
Angst haben vor
  afraid, be afraid of
anhalten stop
Anhänger m trailer
ankommen arrive
Ankunft f arrival
Anlasser m starter (car)
Anlegestelle f mooring
Anmeldeformular n
  registration form
anmelden register (vb)
Anproberaum m
  fitting room
anprobieren try on
Anruf m call (n),
  telephone call
anschauen look at
Anschlagbrett n notice
  board

Anschluss m extension
Anschlussflug m
  connecting flight
ansteckend infectious
anstehen queue (vb)
Anstellung f job
antik ancient, antique
Antwort f answer,
  reply (n)
antworten reply (vb)
Anzahlung f deposit
Anzeige f advert,
  advertisement
anziehen dress (vb)
Anzug m suit (for a
  man)
Apfelsine f orange
Apfelwein m cider
Apotheke f pharmacy
Apotheker m chemist
Apothekerin f chemist
Arbeit f work (n)
arbeiten work (vb)
arbeitslos unemployed
arm poor
Armband n bracelet
Armbanduhr f
  (wrist)watch (n)
Arzt m doctor
Ärztin f doctor
Arztpraxis f doctor's
  surgery
Ast m branch
atmen breathe
auch too, also
auf in, on (position), up
Auf Wiedersehen
  goodbye

GERMAN → ENGLISH

GERMAN → ENGLISH

Aufführung f play, show (n)
aufladen recharge
auflegen hang up (telephone)
auflisten list (vb)
aufmachen open
aufmerken note (vb)
aufregend exciting
aufschliessen unlock
aufschrauben unscrew
aufstehen get up
aufwachen wake up
Aufzug m elevator, lift
Auge n eye
Augen-Make-up-Entferner m eye make-up remover
Augentropfen pl eye drops
aus off (switch), from, out
Ausflug m excursion
Ausfuhr f export
ausfüllen fill in
Ausgang m exit
ausgeben spend
ausgezeichnet excellent
Auskunft f enquiry desk, information
Ausland, im abroad
Ausländer m foreigner
Ausländerin f foreigner
ausländisch foreign
auspacken unpack
Auspuffrohr n exhaust pipe

ausrufen page (vb)
Ausrüstung f equipment
ausschalten switch off, turn off
Ausschlag m rash
ausschliessen exclude, lock out
Ausschluss m suspension (from club, school, etc.)
ausser except
aussergewöhnlich extraordinary
ausserhalb outside
Aussicht f view
aussprechen pronounce
aussteigen get off
Ausstellung f exhibition
Austausch m exchange
Ausverkauf m sale
Ausweis m identity card
Auto n car
Auto-Ersatzteile f car parts
Autobahn f freeway, motorway
Autofähre f car ferry
Automat m vending machine
Autonummer f registration number
Autoschlüssel f car keys
Autovermietung f car hire

Autowaschanlage f
  car-wash

B
Babynahrung f baby
  food
Bach m stream
Bäckerei f bakery
Bad n bath
Badeanzug m
  swimming costume
Bademantel m
  dressing gown
Badezimmer n
  bathroom
Bahnhof m station,
  railway station
Bahnsteig m platform
Bahnübergang m level
  crossing
Baiser n meringue
bald soon
Balkon m balcony
Band n ribbon, strap
Bargeld n cash
Bart m beard
bauen build
Bauer m farmer
Bäuerin f farmer
Bauernhaus n farm-
  house
Bauernhof m farm
Baum m tree
Baumarkt m DIY shop
Baumwolle f cotton
Bayern Bavaria
bedeuten mean (sense)

Bedienung f service
  charge
beenden finish, end (vb)
Beerdigung f funeral
befestigen fasten
behalten keep
behindert disabled,
  handicapped
bei Bewusstsein
  conscious
beide both
Beilage f side dish,
  supplement
Bein n leg
beinahe nearly, almost
Beispiel n example
beitreten join
bekommen get
Belag m filling
  (sandwich)
belästigen annoy
belegtes Brot n
  sandwich
Belichtung f exposure
  (film)
beliebt popular
bellen bark (vb)
benötigen require
benutzen use
Benzin n fuel, gas,
  petrol
Benzinkanister m
  petrol can
bequem comfortable
bereit ready
Berg m mountain
Bergsteigen n
  mountaineering

GERMAN → ENGLISH

Bergwacht f mountain rescue
Bericht m report (n)
berichten report (vb)
Berliner m doughnut
Bernstein m amber
Beruf m occupation
Beruhigungsmittel n tranquillizer
berühmt famous
beschädigen damage (vb)
beschäftigt busy
Bescheinigung f certificate
beschreiben describe
Beschreibung f description
Beschwerde f complaint
beschweren complain
Besen m broom
besetzt engaged (telephone), occupied (toilet)
besonders especially
besorgt worried
Besprechung f meeting
besser better
bestätigen confirm
Bestätigung f confirmation
Besteck n cutlery
bestellen order (vb)
Bestellung f order (n)
bestimmt definitely
Besuch m visit (n)
besuchen visit (vb)

Besucher m visitor
Besucherin f visitor
Besuchszeit f visiting hours
beten pray
Betrag m amount
betrunken drunk
Bett n bed
Bettbezug m duvet cover
Bettdecke f quilt
Bevölkerung f population
bewegen move
Bewohner m resident
Bewohnerin f resident
bewusstlos unconscious
bezahlen pay
bezahlt paid
Bezahlung f payment
Bezirk m district
BH m bra
Bibliothek f library
biegen bend (vb)
Biene f bee
Bild n picture
Bilderrahmen m picture frame
Bildschirm m screen (n, TV)
billig cheap
billiger cheaper
Billigtarif m cheap rate
bin (ich bin) am (I am)
Bio(gemüse) n organic (vegetables)

Bioladen m health food shop
Birne f pear
bis by (time), till, until
Biss m bite (n)
bisschen little (bit)
bitte please
Bitte f request (n)
Blase f blister
Blasenentzündung f cystitis
blass pale
Blatt n leaf
blau blue
Blei n lead (metal)
bleiben remain, stay
Bleichmittel n bleach
bleifrei lead-free
bleifreies Benzin n unleaded petrol
Bleistift m pencil
blind blind (adj)
Blinddarm- entzündung f appendicitis
Blinker m indicator
Blitz m lightning
Blitzlicht n flash
blond fair (hair colour)
Blume f flower
Bluse f blouse
Blut n blood
Blutdruck m blood pressure
bluten bleed
Bluterguss m bruise
blutig bloody, rare (steak)

Boden m floor, ground
Bodensee m Lake Constance
Bohne f bean
Bohrer m drill (n)
Boot n boat
Bootsfahrt f boat trip
Bordkarte f boarding card
borgen borrow
Botschaft f embassy
Bouillon f stock (n, soup)
braten fry
Bratpfanne f frying pan
Brauch m custom, tradition
brauchen need (vb)
Brauerei f brewery
braun brown
Bräune f tan
Braut f bride
Bräutigam m bridegroom
brechen break
Bremse f brake (n)
bremsen brake (vb)
Bremsflüssigkeit f brake fluid
Bremslicht n brake light
brennen burn (vb)
Brief m letter
Brieffreund m penfriend
Brieffreundin f penfriend

GERMAN → ENGLISH

Briefkasten m letterbox, post box

Briefmarke f postage stamp

Briefpapier n writing paper

Brieftasche f wallet

Briefträger m postman

Briefträgerin f postwoman

Brille f eyeglasses, glasses, spectacles

bringen bring

Brise f breeze

Bronchitis f bronchitis

Brosche f brooch

Broschüre f brochure

Brot n bread

Brötchen n bread roll

Brotlaib m loaf of bread

Bruch m hernia

Brücke f bridge

Bruder m brother

Brühe f broth, stock

Brüssel Brussels

Brust f breast, chest

Buch n book

buchen reserve, book (vb)

Buchhandlung f bookshop

buchstabieren spell (vb, letters)

Bucht f bay

Buchung f reservation, booking

Bügelbrett n ironing board

bügeln iron (vb)

Bürger m citizen

Bürgerin f citizen

Bürgersteig m pavement, sidewalk

Büro n office

Bürste f brush

Bus m bus, coach

Busch m bush

Bushaltestelle f bus stop

Butter f butter

C

Campingplatz m camp site

CD-Spieler m CD player

Celsius Centigrade

Champagner m champagne

Charterflug m charter flight

Check-in m check-in

chemische Reinigung f dry cleaner's

China China

Chips f chips, crisps

Chor m choir

Cola f Coke

Computer m computer

Creme f cream

D

da there

Dach n roof

Dachboden m attic

Dachgepäckträger m
roof-rack
Dachziegel m shingle
Dame f lady
Damenbinden f
sanitary pads
Damenkleidung f
ladies' wear
Damentoilette f ladies'
toilet
Dampf m steam
danach afterwards
Dänemark Denmark
dankbar grateful
danken thank
darauf bestehen insist
darf may
das that, the
das ist schade it's a
pity
dass (so) that
dasselbe same
Datei f data, file
Datteln f dates (fruit)
Datum n date
Dauerwelle f perm
Daumen m thumb
Decke f blanket
Deckel m cap, lid
defekt faulty
dein your
denken think
Denkmal n monument
der m the
Desinfektionsmittel n
disinfectant
deutsch German (adj)

Deutsche/r f/m
German (n)
Dezember m
December
Dia n slide (n, film)
Diabetiker diabetic
Diamant m diamond
Diät f diet
dick fat, thick
die f the
die pl the
Dieb m thief
Diebstahl m theft
Diele f entrance hall
Dienst m service
(e.g. in army)
Dienstreise f business
trip
dies this
diese/r/s f/m/n this,
that
diese Woche this week
Diesel m diesel
Ding n thing
direkt direct
Diskette f disk (for
computer)
Dokumente pl
documents
Dolmetscher m
interpreter
Dolmetscherin f
interpreter
Dom m cathedral
Donner m thunder
Donnerstag m
Thursday

GERMAN → ENGLISH

Doppelbett n double bed

doppelt double

Doppelzimmer n double room

Dorf n village

Dorn m thorn

dort there, over there

Dose f can, tin

Dosenöffner m can opener, tin opener

Drachenfliegen n hang-gliding

Draht m wire

Drahtseilbahn f cable car

draussen outdoors, outside

dreckig filthy

drehen turn

dringend urgent

drinnen indoors

Droge f drug

Druck m pressure

drucken print (vb)

Drucksache f printed matter

du you (familiar)

dumm stupid

dunkel dark

dünn thin

durch through

Durchfall m diarrhoea

Durchschnitt m average

Durchzug m draught

durstig thirsty

Dusche f shower (n)

duschen shower (vb)

Dutzend n dozen

E

Ebbe f low tide

echt genuine, real

Ecke f corner

EG f EC

Ehefrau f wife

Ehemann m husband

Ehering m wedding ring

ehrlich honest

Ei n egg

Eiche f oak

eifersüchtig jealous

Eigelb n egg yolk

eigenartig odd, peculiar

Eigentümer m owner

Eile f hurry (n)

eilen hurry, rush (vb)

Eimer m bucket, pail

ein anderes another

ein Foto machen to take a photo

ein paar a few

ein weiteres another

Einbahnstrasse f one-way street

Einbrecher m burglar

Einbruch m burglary, break-in

eine/r f/m one

einfach plain, simple

einfache Fahrkarte single (one-way) ticket

Eingang m entrance

Eingriff m surgical procedure

einige some
Einkaufswagen m
shopping trolley
Einkaufszentrum n
shopping centre
einladen invite
Einladung f invitation
einlaufen shrink,
coming in (ship/train)
einlösen cash in,
redeem
einmal once
eins one
einschalten switch on
einschliessen lock in
einsteigen get on/in
Eintopf m stew
eintragen register (vb)
eintreten enter
Eintrittsgebühr f
entrance fee
Eintrittspreis m admission fee, entrance fee
Einweichlösung f
soaking solution
einwickeln wrap up
Einzel single
Einzelbett n single bed
Einzelheiten pl details
Einzelzimmer n single
room
Eis n ice, ice cream
Eisbahn f skating rink
Eisen n iron (n, metal)
Eisenbahn f railway
Eisenhändler m ironmonger's

Eisenwarenhandlung f
hardware shop
Eiskaffee m iced coffee
ekelhaft revolting
Elektriker m electrician
elektrisch electric
Elektrizität f electricity
Ell(en)bogen m elbow
Eltern pl parents
Empfang m reception
Empfänger m receiver
Empfangschef m
receptionist
Empfangsdame f
receptionist
empfehlen recommend
Ende n end (n)
Endstation f terminal
Endsumme f total, sum
eng narrow, tight
England England
Engländer m
Englishman
Engländerin f
Englishwoman
englisch English
Enkel m grandson
Enkelin f granddaughter
entdecken discover
Ente f duck
Entfernung f distance
entgegengesetzt
opposite
enthalten hold, contain
entkommen escape
entscheiden decide
Entscheidung f
decision

entschuldigen Sie, bitte excuse me, please

Entschuldigung f apology

Entschuldigung! sorry!

enttäuscht disappointed

entweder ... oder either ... or

entwickeln develop

Entzündung f inflammation

Epileptiker m epileptic

Epileptikerin f epileptic

er he

erbitten request (vb)

erbrechen vomit

Erbse f pea

Erdbeben n earthquake

Erdbeere f strawberry

Erde f earth

Erdgeschoss n ground floor, basement

Erdnuss f peanut

Erdrutsch m landslide

erfahren experienced

erfreut pleased

erhalten obtain

erhältlich available

erinnern remember

Erkältung f cold (n, i.e. illness)

erkennen realize, recognize

erklären explain

erlauben allow

Ermässigung f concession, reduction

ernst serious

Ernte f harvest

Ersatzreifen m spare tyre/wheel

Ersatzteil n spare part

Ersatzteile f car parts

erschöpft exhausted

erstaunlich amazing, astonishing

Erste m/f first

Erste Hilfe f first aid

Erste Klasse f first class

Erster first

Erster Stock m first floor

Erwachsene m adult

erwähnen mention

erwarten expect

es it

es schneit it is snowing

es tut weh it's sore

essen eat

Essen n food

Essen zum Mitnehmen take-away food

Essig m vinegar

Esslöffel m tablespoon

Esszimmer n dining room

Estland Estonia

Etage f floor

Etikett n label

etwas something, anything

EU f EU (European Union)

Eule f owl
Europa Europe
europäisch European
evangelisch
  protestant (adj)
Explosion f explosion
Export m export
Express express (mail)

F

Fabrik f factory
Fächer m fan
Faden m thread
Fahne f flag
Fähre f ferry
fahren drive, go (by car)
Fahrer m driver
Fahrerin f driver
Fahrgast m passenger
Fahrkarte f ticket
Fahrkartenschalter m
  ticket office (bus, train)
Fahrplan m timetable
Fahrpreis m fare
Fahrrad n bicycle, cycle
Fahrzeug n vehicle
fallen fall (vb)
fällig due
falsch false, wrong
Fälschung f fake,
  counterfeit
Falten pl wrinkles
falten fold (paper)
Familie f family
Fan m fan
fangen catch
Farbe f colour, dye (n),
  paint (n)

färben dye (vb)
farbenblind colour blind
Farbfilm m colour film
Fass n barrel
Fassbier n draught beer
fast almost, nearly
faul lazy
Fax n fax
Februar m February
Feder f spring (metal),
  feather
Federbett n duvet
Federung f suspension
  (of car)
Fehler m fault, error,
  mistake
Feiertag m holiday
Feile f file (metal)
Feld n field
Felsen m cliff, rock
Fenster n window
Fensterladen m shutter
Fensterplatz m window
  seat
Ferngespräch n long-
  distance call
Fernglas n binoculars
Fernseher m television
  set
Ferse m heel (foot)
fertig ready
Fest n festival
Festplatte f hard disk
feststecken stuck
Festung t fortress
Fete f party (celebration)
fett fatty
fettarm low fat

GERMAN → ENGLISH

fettig greasy

feucht damp, humid

Feuchtigkeitscreme f moisturizer

Feuer n fire, cigarette lighter

feuerfest ovenproof

Feuerlöscher m fire extinguisher

Feuerwehr f fire brigade

Feuerzeug n cigarette lighter

Fieber n temperature, fever

Filet n fillet

Filiale f branch

Film m film

Filmentwicklung f film processing

Filter m filter

finden find

Finger m finger

Firma f company, firm

Fisch m fish (n)

fischen fish (vb)

Fischhandlung f fishmonger's

Fitness-Studio n gym

FKK-Strand m nudist beach

flach flat (adj)

Flagge f flag

Flasche f bottle

Flaschenöffner m bottle opener

Fleck m stain (n)

Fleisch n meat

Fleischer m butcher

flicken mend

Fliege f bow tie

Fliege f fly (n)

fliegen fly (vb)

fliessend fluent

Flitterwochen f honeymoon

Floh m flea

fluchen swear, curse

Fluchwort n swear word

Flug m flight

Flughafen m airport

Flugschein m open ticket

Flugticket n air ticket

Flugzeug n aeroplane, plane

Flur m corridor

Fluss m river

Flut f flood (n), high tide

folgen follow

Fön m hairdryer

fönen blow-dry

Forelle f trout

formell formal

Formular n form (n, official)

Foto n photo

Fotokopie f photocopy

Foyer n lobby

Frage f question

fragen ask

Frankreich France

Franzose m Frenchman

Französin f French-woman

französisch French

Frau Mrs/Ms
Frau f woman
Fräulein n Miss
frei free
freiberuflich freelance
freiberuflich tätig self-
employed
freies Zimmer vacancy
(B&B, hotel)
Freistelle f vacancy (job)
Freitag m Friday
Freizeichen n dialling
tone
Fremde/r f/m stranger
Fremdenführer/in m/f
guide
Freude f joy
Freund m friend,
boyfriend
Freundin f friend,
girlfriend
freundlich friendly
Friedhof m cemetery
frisch fresh
Frischhaltefolie f cling
film, clingwrap
Friseur m hairdresser
froh glad
Frohe Ostern! Happy
Easter!
Frohes Neues Jahr!
Happy New Year!
Frosch m frog
Frost m frost
Frucht f fruit
Fruchtsaft m fruit juice
Frühling m spring
(season)

Frühstück n breakfast
Fuchs m fox
fühlen feel
führen lead (vb)
Führerschein m
licence, driving licence
Führung f guided tour
füllen fill (vb)
Füllung f filling (tooth)
Fundbüro n lost
property
funktionieren work
(machine)
für for
furchtbar awful
Fuss m foot
Fussball m football,
soccer
Fussballspiel n football
match, soccer match
Füsse f feet
Fussgänger m
pedestrian
**Fussgänger-
übergang** m
pedestrian crossing
Fussweg m footpath
füttern feed

G
Gabel f fork
Gabelung f fork (road)
Galerie f gallery
Gallone f gallon
Gang m aisle, course
(meals), gear, gait
Gangplatz m aisle seat
Gans f goose

ganz whole
Garage f garage
Garantie f guarantee
Garderobe f cloakroom
Gardine f curtain
Garnele f prawn
Garten m garden
Gas n gas
Gasflasche f gas cylinder
Gasherd m gas cooker
Gaspedal n accelerator
Gasse f (narrow) lane
Gast m guest
Gastfreundschaft f hospitality
Gasthaus n inn
Gebäck n biscuits, pastry
Gebäude n building
geben give
Gebiet n region
Gebiss n dentures
geboren born
gebraten fried
Gebrauchs-anweisung f user manual
gebraucht second-hand
gebrochen broken
Geburt f birth
Geburtsdatum n date of birth
Geburtstag m birthday
Geburtstags-geschenk n birthday present

Geburtstagskarte f birthday card
Geburtsurkunde f birth certificate
Gedeckkosten f cover charge
gedeckter Kuchen pie
Gefahr f danger
gefährlich dangerous
gefallen like (vb)
Gefängnis n prison
Gefriertruhe f freezer
gefroren frozen
gefüllt stuffed
gegen against
Gegend f area
gegenüber opposite
gegrillt grilled
gehen go (on foot), walk
Gehirnerschütterung f concussion
gelb yellow, amber
Gelbe Seiten pl Yellow Pages
Gelbsucht f jaundice
Geld n money
Geldautomat m auto-teller, cash dispenser
Geldbörse f purse
Geldschein m note (n, paper money)
Geldstrafe f fine (n)
gelegentlich occasionally
Gelenk n joint
gemacht made
Gemälde n painting

gemein mean, nasty
Gemüse n vegetables
Gemüsehändler m greengrocer
genau absolutely, exactly, accurate
Genehmigung f licence, permit
Genf Geneva
Genick n neck
geniessen enjoy
genug enough
geöffnet open
Gepäck n baggage, luggage
Gepäckablage f luggage rack
Gepäckanhänger m luggage tag
Gepäckausgabe f baggage reclaim
Gepäckträger m porter
Gepäckwagen m trolley, luggage trolley
geplatzt burst
gerade straight
geradeaus straight on
geraspelt grated
geräucherter Lachs smoked salmon
gerecht fair, just
Gericht n dish, court (of law)
gerieben grated
gerissen torn
Geruch m smell (n)

Geschäft n business, deal, shop, store
Geschäftsführer m manager
Geschäftsführerin f manager
geschehen happen
Geschenk n gift, present
Geschenkpapier n wrapping paper
Geschichte f history, story
geschieden divorced
Geschirr n crockery
Geschirrspül-maschine f dishwasher
Geschirrtuch n tea towel
Geschlecht n sex, gender
Geschlechts-krankheit f venereal disease
geschlossen shut, closed
Geschmack m flavour
geschützt sheltered
Geschwindigkeit f speed
Geschwindigkeits-begrenzung f speed limit
geschwollen swollen
Geschwür n ulcer
Gesetz n law

GERMAN → ENGLISH

GERMAN → ENGLISH

gesetzlicher Feiertag public holiday
Gesicht n face
gestern yesterday
gestern Abend last night
gestern Nacht last night
gestohlen stolen
gestreift striped, brushed against
gesund healthy
Getränk n drink (n)
getrennt separate
Getriebe n gearbox
Gewicht n weight
gewinnen win
gewiss certainly, sure
Gewitter n thunderstorm
gewöhnlich usual
Gewürz n seasoning, spice
Gezeiten pl tides
giessen pour
Gift n poison
giftig poisonous
Gipfel m peak, summit
Gips m plaster cast
Gitarre f guitar
Glas n glass, jar
Glatteis n black ice
glauben believe
Gletscher m glacier
Glocke f bell
Glück m luck
glücklich lucky, happy

glücklicherweise fortunately
Glückwunsch m congratulation
Glühbirne f light bulb
Gold n gold
Golfplatz m golf course
Golfschläger m golf club
gotisch Gothic
Gott m God
Grad m degree
Gramm n gram
Grammatik f grammar
Gras n grass
gratis free
grau grey
Grenze f border
Griechenland Greece
griechisch Greek
Griff m handle
Grippe f flu
gross big, large
grossartig grand, great
Grossbritannien Britain, Great Britain
Grösse f size
Grosseltern pl grandparents
Grossmutter f grandmother
Grossvater m grandfather
grosszügig generous
grün green
Gruppe f group, party

Gruss m greeting
gültig valid
Gummi n/m elastic, rubber
günstig convenient
Gurke f cucumber
Gürtel m belt
Gürtelrose f shingles
Gürteltasche f money belt
gut good, nice, well
gutaussehend handsome
Gute Nacht good night
Guten Abend good evening
Guten Morgen good morning
Guten Tag good day, How do you do?
Gutschein m voucher

H
Haarbürste f hairbrush
Haare pl hair
Haarschnitt m haircut
haben have
hacken chop (vb)
Hackfleisch n minced meat
Hafen m port, harbour
Hafer m oats
Haftpflicht-versicherung f third-party insurance
Hagel m hail
halb half (adj)

halbdurch (Fleisch) medium rare (meat)
Halbinsel f peninsula
halbtrocken (Wein) medium dry (wine)
Hälfte f half (n)
Hallenbad n indoor pool
Hals m neck, throat
Halskette f necklace
Halspastillen fpl throat lozenges
Halsschmerzen fpl sore throat
Haltbarkeitsdatum n sell-by date
halten hold, stop
Hamburger m hamburger, person from Hamburg
Hammelfleisch n mutton
Hammer m hammer
Hand f hand
Handbremse f handbrake
handgearbeitet handmade
Handgelenk n wrist
Handgepäck n hand luggage
Handschaltung f manual (car)
Handschuhe pl gloves
Handtasche f handbag
Handtuch n towel
Handwerk n craft
Handy n mobile phone

GERMAN → ENGLISH

Harke f rake
hart hard
Hase m hare
Haselnüsse fpl hazelnuts
hässlich ugly
Haube f bonnet (of car), hood
häufig frequent
Haupt- main
Hauptgang m main course (meal)
Hauptpostamt n main post office
Hauptschalter m mains switch
Hauptstadt f capital city
Hauptstrasse f main road
Haus n house
Hausarbeit f housework
Hausmeister m caretaker, suprintendent
Hausschuhe pl slippers
Haustier n pet
Hauswein m house wine, table wine
Haut f skin
Hebel m lever
Heftpflaster n sticking plaster
heilig holy
Heiligabend Christmas Eve
Heimweh n homesickness
heiss hot

heizen heat (vb)
Heizkörper m radiator (in room)
Heizung f heating
helfen help
hell bright
helles Bier n lager
Hemd n shirt
Herbst m autumn, fall
Herd m cooker, oven
hereinkommen come in
hergestellt made
Hering m tent peg, herring
Herr Mr
Herrenbekleidung f men's wear
Herrenfrisör m barber
Herrenschneider m tailor
Herrentoilette f gents' toilet
Herz n heart
Herzanfall m heart attack
Herzschrittmacher m pacemaker
Heuschnupfen m hay fever
heute today
heute Abend tonight
heute Morgen this morning
hier here, over here
hier entlang this way
Hilfe! Help!
Himbeere f raspberry

Himmel m sky
hinkommen get to
hinlegen lie down
hinstellen put, stand up
hinten, hinter behind
hinterlassen leave (vb)
Hirnhautentzündung f
  meningitis
historisch historic
Hitze f heat (n)
hoch high, tall
Höchstrate f peak rate
Hochzeit f wedding
Hochzeitsgeschenk n
  wedding present
hoffen hope (vb)
hoffentlich hopefully
Hoffnung f hope (n)
höflich polite
Höhe f height
hoher Blutdruck high
  blood pressure
Höhle f cave
holen fetch
holländisch Dutch
Holz n wood
Holzkohle f charcoal
homosexuell gay
Honig m honey
hören hear
Hörer m telephone
  receiver
Hörgerät n hearing aid
Hose f trousers
Hosen f pants
hübsch pretty
Hubschrauber m
  helicopter

Hüfte f hip
Hühnchen n chicken
Hummer m lobster
Humor m humour
Hund m dog
hungrig hungry
Hupe f hooter, horn (car)
husten cough (vb)
Husten m cough (n)
Hustensaft m cough
  mixture
Hut m hat

I
ich I
Idee f idea
ihm/ihn him
ihr/sie her
im in
im Ausland abroad
im Voraus advance,
  in advance
Imbiss m snack
immer always, ever
Immobilienmakler m
  estate agent
in in, into
in der Nähe nearby
in Ordnung all right, OK
in Verbindung treten
  contact (vb)
inbegriffen included
Inder/in m/f Indian (n)
Indien m India
Indisch Indian (adj)
Infektion f infection
Ingenieur m engineer
Ingenieurin f engineer

Inland n interior
(of country)
innen inside
Innenstadt f city centre
Insekt n insect
Insektenschutzmittel n
insect repellent
Insektenstich m insect
bite
Insel f island
insgesamt altogether
Insulin m insulin
intelligent intelligent
interessant interesting
international inter-
national
Ire m Irishman
irgendwo somewhere
Irin f Irishwoman
irisch Irish
Irland Ireland
Irrtum m mistake
ist is
Italien Italy
Italiener m Italian (n)
Italienerin f Italian (n)
italienisch Italian (adj)

J
ja yes
Jacht f yacht
Jacke f jacket
Jagderlaubnis f
hunting permit
Jagdschein m hunting
permit
jagen hunt
Jahr n year

Jahrestag m
anniversary
Jahreszeit f season
Jahrhundert n century
jährlich annual
Jalousie f blind (n, for
window)
Januar m January
jede/jeder/jedes f/m/n
each, every, everyone
jemand someone,
somebody
jene those
jene/r/s that
jenseits beyond
jetzt now
joggen jog
jubeln cheer (vb)
jucken itch
Jude m Jew
Jüdin f Jewess
jüdisch Jewish
Jugendherberge f
youth hostel
Juli m July
jung young
Junge m boy
Juni m June
Juwelier m jeweller

K
Kabel n electrical lead
Kabeljau m cod (fish)
Kabine f cabin
Kaffee m coffee
Kai m quay
Kakao m cocoa
Kakerlake f cockroach

Kalb n calf
Kalbfleisch n veal
kalt cold (adj)
Kamm m comb
kämpfen fight (vb)
Kanada Canada
Kanal m canal, channel
Kaninchen n rabbit
Kante f edge, rim
Kanu n canoe
Kanzler m prime minister
Kapelle f chapel, band
Kapital n capital (n, money)
kaputt out of order, broken
Kapuze f hood (on a jacket)
Karfreitag Good Friday
Karotte f carrot
Karte f card, ticket
Kartoffel f potato
Kartoffelpüree n mashed potatoes
Karton m box, carton
Käse m cheese
Kasse f cash desk, till
Kassette f cassette, tape
Kassettenrecorder m tape recorder
Kassierer(in) m/f cashier
Kastanie f chestnut
Kasten m chest
Katastrophe f disaster

Kater m hangover, male cat
Kathedrale f cathedral
katholisch Catholic
Katze f cat
kaufen buy
Kaufhaus n department store
Kaugummi n/m chewing gum
kaum hardly
Kehle f throat
Keilriemen m fan belt
kein no
keine/r no-one
Keks m biscuit
Keller m cellar
Kellner m waiter
Kellnerin f waitress
kennen know
Kennzeichen n registration number
Kerze f candle
Kfz-Versicherung f car insurance
kicken kick (vb)
Kiefer m jaw
Kilo, Kilogramm n kilo, kilogram
Kilometer m kilometre
Kind n child
Kinderbett n cot
Kinderhort m crèche
Kinderkarre f pushchair
Kindermädchen n nanny, au pair
Kindersitz m child car seat

GERMAN → ENGLISH

Kinderstube f nursery
Kinderstuhl m high chair
Kinderwagen m pram
Kinn n chin
Kino n cinema
Kiosk m kiosk
Kirche f church
Kirmes f (church) fair (n)
Kirsche f cherry
Kissen n cushion
Kissenbezug m pillowcase
klar clear
Klärgrube f septic tank
Klasse f class
Klavier n piano
Klebeband n adhesive tape
kleben stick
Klebstoff m glue
Kleider pl clothes
Kleiderbügel m coat hanger
Kleiderschrank m wardrobe
klein little, small
klemmen stuck
Klempner m plumber
klettern climb
Klimaanlage f air conditioning
Klingel f doorbell
klingeln ring (vb)
Klinik f clinic
klopfen knock
Kloster n monastery
klug clever

Knie n knee
Knoblauch m garlic
Knöchel m ankle
Knochen m bone
Knochenbruch m fracture
Knolle f bulb (plant)
Knopf m button
Koch/Köchin m/f chef, cook (n)
kochen boil, cook (vb)
Kochnische f kitchenette
Kochrezept n recipe
Kode f code
Köder m bait
koffeinfrei decaffeinated
Koffer m case, suitcase, trunk
Kofferkuli m luggage trolley
Kofferraum m boot (of car), trunk
Kohl m cabbage
Kohle f coal (also slang for money)
Kokosnuss f coconut
Kola f Coke
Kollege/Kollegin m/f colleague
Köln Cologne
komisch funny
kommen come
Kommode f chest of drawers
Komödie f comedy
Kompass m compass

Komponist/in m/f composer
Konditorei f cake shop
Kondom m/n condom
Konferenz f conference
Konfitüre f jam
König m king
Königin f queen
königlich royal
können can
könnte could, might
konnte nicht couldn't
Konsulat n consulate
Kontakte pl points (car)
Kontaktlinse f contact lens
Konto n account
kontrollieren check
Konzert n concert
Kopf m head
Kopfhörer pl headphones, earphones
Kopfkissen n pillow
Kopfkissenbezug m pillowcase
Kopfsalat m lettuce
Kopfschmerzen pl headache
Kopie f copy (n)
kopieren copy (vb)
Korb m basket
Korken m cork
Korkenzieher m corkscrew
Körper m body
Körperpuder n talcum powder

Kosmetiksalon m beauty salon
kosten taste, cost (vb)
Kosten pl cost (n)
köstlich delicious
Kostüm n suit (for a woman)
Krabbe f shrimp
Krabben pl shrimps
Kragen m collar
Krampf m cramp
krank ill, sick
Krankenhaus n hospital
Krankenpfleger m male nurse
Krankenpflegerin f nurse
Krankenversicherung f medical insurance
Krankenwagen m ambulance
Krankheit f disease, illness
Krapfen m doughnut
kratzen scratch (vb)
Kratzer m scratch (n)
kraus curly
Kräuter f herbs
Kräutertee m herbal tea
Krawatte f tie
Krebs m cancer, crab
Kreditkarte f charge card, credit card
Kreis m circle
Kreisverkehr m roundabout
Kreuz n cross (n)
Kreuzfahrt f cruise

GERMAN → ENGLISH

GERMAN → ENGLISH

Kreuzung f crossroads, intersection, junction
Kreuzworträtsel n crossword puzzle
Krieg m war
Kristall m crystal
Krone f crown
Krücken pl crutches
Krug m jug
Krustentiere pl shellfish
Küche f kitchen
Kuchen m cake
Küchengeräte pl cooking utensils
Küchenschabe f cockroach
Kugelschreiber m ballpoint pen
Kuh f cow
kühl cool
Kühler m radiator (car)
Kühlschrank m fridge
Kühltasche/box f cool bag/box
Kunde m client, customer
Kundin f client
Kunst f art
Kunstfaser f man-made fibre
Kunstgewerbe n craft
Künstler m artist
künstliches Hüftgelenk n hip replacement
Kupplung f clutch
Kurierdienst m courier service

Kurort m spa
Kurs m course, rate of exchange
Kurve f bend (n)
kurz short
kürzlich recently
kurzsichtig short-sighted
Kusine f cousin (female)
Kuss m kiss
Küste f coast, seaside
Küstenwache f coastguard

L
lächeln smile
lachen laugh
lächerlich ridiculous
Lachs m salmon
Laden m store
Lagerhalle f warehouse
Laken n sheet
Lamm n lamb
Lampe f lamp
Land n land (n), country
landen land (vb)
Landkarte f map
Landschaft f countryside, scenery
lang long, tall
langsam slow, slowly
langweilig boring
Lappen m cloth, rag
Lärm m noise
lassen let
Laster m truck
Lastwagen (LKW) m lorry

Latschen pl flip flops
Lauch m leek
laut loud, noisy
Lawine f avalanche
Leben n life
leben live (vb)
**Lebensmittel-
 geschäft n** food shop
Lebensversicherung f
 life insurance
Leber f liver
lebhaft lively
Leck n leak (n)
Leder n leather
ledig single
leer empty
leere Batterie f flat
 battery
Lehrer m teacher
Lehrerin f teacher
leicht easy, light
Leihbücherei f library
leihen borrow, lend
Leim m glue
Leinen n linen
leise quiet (adv)
Leiter f ladder
Leitung f line
 (telephone)
lenken steer
Lenkrad n steering
 wheel
lernen learn
lesbisch lesbian
lesen read
Lettland Latvia
letzte/s last

letzte Woche last
 week
Letzte/r f/m last
Leute pl people
Licht n light (n)
Lichtmaschine f
 dynamo
Lidschatten m eye
 shadow
liebe/r dear (form of
 address)
Liebe f love (n)
lieben love (vb)
Lieblings- favourite
Lied n song
liefern deliver
Lieferwagen m van
liegen lie down
Liegestuhl m deck
 chair
Liegewagen m
 couchette
Likör m liqueur
Limonade f lemonade
Limone f lime
Lineal n ruler (for
 measuring)
Linie f line (on paper)
links left
Linkshänder m left-
 handed man
Linkshänderin f left-
 handed woman
Linse f lens
Linsen pl lentils
Lippenstift m lipstick
Liste f list (n)
Litauen Lithuania

165

Liter m litre
Loch n hole
Löffel m spoon
Lohn m wage
Lorbeerblatt n bay leaf
lose loose
löslich soluble
Löwe m lion
Luft f air
Luftkissenboot n hovercraft
Luftpost f airmail
Lüge f lie (n)
Lunge f lung
Lutscher m lollipop
Luxemburg Luxembourg
Luxus m luxury

M
machen do, make (vb)
macht nichts! (it) doesn't matter
Mädchen n girl
Mädchenname m maiden name
Made f maggot
Magen m stomach
Magenschmerzen pl stomach ache
Magenverstimmung f indigestion
Magnet m magnet
Mahlzeit f meal
Mai m May
malen paint (vb)
manchmal sometimes

Mandarine f tangerine
Mandel f almond
Mandelentzündung f tonsillitis
Mangel m flaw
Mann m man
Männer pl men
männlich male
Mannschaft f team (sport)
Manschettenknöpfe pl cufflinks
Mantel m coat
Marine f navy
marineblau navy blue
Marionettentheater n puppet theatre
Marke f brand, make (n)
Markt m market
Marmelade f jam
Marmor m marble
März m March
Maschine f machine
Masern f measles
Massband n tape measure
Mast m mast
Material n material
Matratze f mattress
Mauer f wall
Maus f mouse
Mayonnaise f mayonnaise
Mechaniker m mechanic
Medien pl media
Medikament n drug
Medizin f medicine

Mehl n flour
mehr more
mehrere several
**Mehrwertsteuer
(MWS)** f value added
tax (VAT)
meiden avoid
Meile f mile
mein my
Meinung f opinion
meistens mostly
Melone f melon
Menge f amount, crowd
Messe f fair (n), mass (n)
messen measure (vb)
Messer n knife
Metall n metal
Meter m metre
Metzger m butcher
mich me
Mietauto n hire car
Miete f rent (n)
mieten rent (vb)
Mietvertrag m lease
Migräne f migraine
Mikrowelle f microwave
Milch f milk
Mineralwasser n
mineral water
Minister/in m/f minister
(politics)
Minute f minute
mir me
mischen mix (vb)
Mischung f mixture
Missverständnis n
misunderstanding
mit by, with

mit Führung guided
(tour)
Mitfahrgelegenheit f
lift (ride)
Mittag m midday, noon
Mittagessen n lunch
Mitte f centre, middle
Mittel n potion
mittel medium
mittelalterlich medieval
mittelgross medium
sized
Mittelmeer n
Mediterranean
Mitternacht f midnight
Mittwoch m
Wednesday
Möbel fpl furniture
Mobiltelefon n mobile
phone
möbliert furnished
möchten want
modisch fashionable
mögen like (vb)
möglich possible
Mohn m poppy
Möhre f carrot
Moment m moment
Monat m month
monatlich monthly
Mond m moon
Montag m Monday
Morgen m morning
morgen tomorrow
morgen Abond
tomorrow evening
morgen Nachmittag
tomorrow afternoon

GERMAN → ENGLISH

morgen Vormittag tomorrow morning
Morgendämmerung f dawn
Morgenrock m dressing gown
Moschee f mosque
Moslime Muslim
moslimisch Muslim (adj)
Motor m engine, motor
Motorboot n motorboat
Motorhaube f bonnet (of car)
Motorrad n motorbike
Motte f moth
Möwe f sea gull
müde sleepy, tired
Müll f refuse (n)
Mülleimer m rubbish bin, trash can
Mülltonne f dustbin
Mumps m mumps
München Munich
Mund m mouth
Mundgeschwür n mouth ulcer
Mundwasser n mouthwash
Münze f coin
Münztelefon n payphone
Muscheln fpl mussels
Museum n museum
Musiker/in m/f musician
Muskel m muscle
muss must
Muster n pattern

Mutter f mother
Mütze f cap

N
nach after, to
Nachbar m neighbour
Nachfrage f enquiry
Nachmittag m afternoon
nachmittags p.m.
Nachname m surname
Nachricht f message
Nachrichten pl news
nächste next
nächste Woche next week
Nacht f night
Nachthemd n nightie
Nachtisch m dessert, pudding
Nadel f needle
Nagel m nail
Nagelbürste f nail brush
Nagelfeile f nail file
Nagellack m nail varnish/polish
Nagellackentferner m nail polish remover
Nagelschere f nail scissors
nahe near
nähen sew, stitch (vb)
Name m name
Narkose f anaesthetic
Nase f nose
nass wet
national national
Natur f nature

natürlich natural
Naturschutzgebiet n
nature reserve
Nebel m fog, mist
neben beside
Neffe m nephew
negativ negative (adj)
Negativ n negative
(n, film)
nehmen take
nein no
**Nervenzusammen-
bruch** m nervous
breakdown
Nest n nest
nett kind
Netz n net, web
neu new
Neujahr n New Year
Neuseeland New
Zealand
Neuseeländer m New
Zealander
Neuseeländerin f New
Zealander
nicht not
nicht da not there, out,
not available
nicht durch underdone
(meat)
nicht gar underdone
Nichte f niece
Nichtraucher non-
smoking, non-smoker
nichts nothing
nie never
Niederlande f
Netherlands

niedrig low
niemand nobody
Niere f kidney
niesen sneeze
noch still
noch ein another
Norden m north
Nordirland Northern
Ireland
Nordsee f North Sea
Norwegen Norway
norwegisch Norwegian
Notausgang m fire exit,
emergency exit
Notfall m emergency
Notiz f note (n)
Notizbuch n notebook
Notizpapier n notepaper
notwendig necessary
November m
November
nüchtern sober
null zero
Nummer f number
Nummernschild n
number plate
nur just, only
Nürnberg Nuremberg
Nuss f nut
nützlich useful

O
oben top, upstairs
oben ohne topless
oberhalb above
oberstes Stockwerk
top floor

GERMAN → ENGLISH

obligatorisch required, obligatory
Obst n fruit
obwohl although
oder or
Ofen m heater
offen open
öffentlich public
Öffnungszeiten fpl opening times
oft often
ohne without
ohnmächtig werden faint (vb)
Ohr n ear
Ohrenschmerzen pl earache
Ohrringe pl earrings
Oktober m October
Öl n oil
Olive f olive
Olivenöl n olive oil
Omelette n omelette
Onkel m uncle
Oper f opera
Operation f operation
Optiker m optician
Orange f orange
Orangenmarmelade f marmalade
Orangensaft m orange juice
Orchester n orchestra
Ordner m file (folder)
örtlich local
Osten m east
Osterei n Easter egg
Ostern Easter

Ostsee f Baltic Sea
Ozean m ocean

P
Paar n **(ein paar)** pair, a couple
packen pack
Packung f carton, package
Paket n packet, parcel
Palast m palace
Panne f breakdown
Papier n paper
Papierservietten f paper napkins
Papiertaschentuch n tissue
Papierwindeln pl disposable diapers/ nappies
Pappe f cardboard
Paprikaschote f pepper (capsicum)
Parfüm n perfume
Park m park (n)
parken park (vb)
Parkett n stalls (theatre)
Parkkralle f wheel clamp
Parkscheibe f parking disc
Parkschein m parking ticket
Parkuhr f parking meter
Partei f party (politics)
Partner m partner
Partnerin f partner
Passagier m passenger

passen fit (vb)
Passierschein m pass
Passkontrolle f pass control
Pastete f pie
Patient m patient
Pauschalreise f package holiday
Pause f interval
Pedale pl pedal
Pelz m fur
Pelzmantel m fur coat
Pension f boarding house, guesthouse
pensioniert retired
per Einschreiben registered mail
perfekt perfect
Periode f period
Perle f pearl
Person f person
Perücke f wig
Pfanne f pan
Pfannkuchen m pancake
Pfarrer m minister (religion)
Pfeffer m pepper (spice)
Pfefferminz m mint (sweet)
Pfeife f pipe
Pferd n horse
Pferderennen n horse racing
Pfirsich m peach
Pflanze f plant
Pflaster n sticking plaster

Pflaume f plum
Pfund n pound
Picknick n picnic
pikant savoury
Pille f pill, tablet
Pilot m pilot
Pilz m mushroom
Pinsel m brush
Pinzette f tweezers
Plakat n poster
Plastik n plastic
Plastiktüte f plastic bag
Platz m place, seat, square (town square)
Plätzchen n cookie
plötzlich suddenly
pochiert poached (egg)
Polen Poland
polieren polish (vb)
Politur f polish (n)
Polizei f police
Polizeiwache f police station
Polizist m policeman
Polizistin f policewoman
polnisch Polish
Pommes frites f chips, French fries
Portier m doorman
Portion f portion
Porto n postage
Portrait n portrait
Portugal Portugal
Portugiese m Portuguese man
Portugiesin f Portuguese woman

GERMAN → ENGLISH

portugiesisch Portuguese (adj)
Portwein m port (wine)
Porzellan n china
Post f mail, post (n)
Postamt n post office
Postanweisung f money order
Postkarte f postcard
Postleitzahl f postal code
Pralinen f chocolates
Praxis f practice (e.g. doctor, lawyer)
Preis m price, prize
Premierminister/in m/f prime minister
Priester m priest
privat private
pro per
Problem n problem
Programm n programme, program
Prosit! cheers!
Prospekt m leaflet
Protestant/in m/f Protestant
provisorisch temporary
Prüfung f examination
Publikum n audience
Puder n powder
Pullover m jumper, pullover, sweater
Pulverkaffee m instant coffee
Pumpe f pump
Punkt m point (n)

Puppe f doll
Pute f turkey

Q
Qualität f quality
Qualle f jellyfish
Quantität f quantity
Quarantäne f quarantine
Quatsch! m Rubbish!
Quelle f fountain
Quittung f receipt

R
R-Gespräch n reverse charge call, collect call
Rabatt m discount
Rad n wheel
Radieschen n radish
Radio n radio
Radweg m cycle track
Rahm m cream
Rahmen m frame
Rand m edge
Rang m circle (theatre)
Rasierapparat m razor
rasieren shave
Rasierklingen pl razor blades
Rasse f race (nation)
raten advise
Rathaus n town hall
Ratte f rat
Rauch m smoke (n)
rauchen smoke (vb)
rauh rough
Rechnung f account, bill, invoice

Rechteck n square (mathematics)
rechts right (direction)
Rechtsanwalt m lawyer
Rechtssteuerung f right-hand drive
reduzieren reduce
Regal n shelf
regeln arrange
Regen m rain (n)
Regenmantel m raincoat
Regierung f government
Register n register (n)
regnen rain (vb)
reich rich (wealthy)
Reich n empire
reichhaltig rich (food)
reif ripe
Reifen m tyre
Reifendruck m tyre pressure
Reifenpanne f flat tyre, puncture
Reihe f row (n), line
Reinigungscreme f cleansing lotion
Reinigungslösung f cleaning solution
Reis m rice
Reise f journey, tour
Reisebüro n travel agent
Reiseführer m guide book
Reisekrankheit f travel sickness

Reiseleiter/in m/f tour guide
reisen travel
Reisepapiere pl travel documents
Reisepass m passport
Reisescheck m traveller's cheque
Reiseveranstalter m tour operator
Reiseveranstalterin f tour operator
Reiseziel n destination
reissen tear (vb)
Reissverschluss m zip
Reiten n horse riding
reiten ride
Rennbahn f race course
Rennen n race (e.g. horse race)
rennen run
Rentner/in m/f senior citizen, pensioner
Reparatur f repair (n)
reparieren fix, mend, repair
reservieren reserve, book (vb)
Reservierung f reservation, booking
Rest m rest, remainder
retten save, rescue (vb)
Rettung f rescue (n)
Rettungsring m life belt
Rettungsschwimmer m life guard
Rezept n prescription, recipe

Rhein m Rhine
Rheumatismus m
 rheumatism
Richter m judge
richtig correct, properly,
 right
Richtung f direction
riechen smell (vb)
Rinde f bark (n, tree)
Rindfleisch n beef
Ring m ring (n)
Rippe f rib
Riss m tear (n)
Rock m skirt
Roggenbrot n rye
 bread
roh raw
Rollo n blind (n)
Rollschuh m roller
 skate (n)
Rollstuhl m wheelchair
Rolltreppe f escalator
Roman m novel
Röntgenaufnahme f
 X-ray
rosa pink
Rose f rose
Rosine f raisin
rostig rusty
rot red
**rote Johannis-
 beeren** fpl
 red currants
Röteln f German
 measles, rubella
Rotwein m red wine
Rouge n blusher
Rücken m back

Rückenschmerzen pl
 backache
Rückerstattung f
 refund
Rückfahrkarte f return
 ticket
Rückgrat n spine
Rucksack m backpack
Rückspiegel m rear-
 view mirror
rückwärts fahren
 reverse (in car)
Rückwärtsgang m
 reverse gear
Ruder n oar, rudder
rudern row (vb)
rufen call (vb)
Ruhe f rest, quiet (n)
ruhig calm
Rühreier pl scrambled
 eggs
Ruine f ruin
Rum m rum
rund round (adj)
Runde f round (n)
Rundfahrt f tour
Rundfunk m radio
Rundgang m guided
 tour
rutschen slip
rutschig slippery

S
Sache f matter
Safe m safe (n)
Saft m juice
sagen tell, say (vb)
Sahne f cream

Salat m salad

Salatsauce f salad dressing

Salbe f ointment

Salz n salt

sammeln collect

Samstag m Saturday

Sand m sand

Sandalen pl sandals

Sänger/in m/f singer

Sattel m saddle

Satz m sentence, set

sauber clean (adj)

säubern clean (vb)

Sauce (Sosse) f gravy, sauce

sauer sour

Sauger m teat (of bottle)

Säugling m baby

Säuglingstragetasche f carry-cot

Saum m hem

säurebindendes Mittel antacid

Schachspiel n chess

Schachtel f box

schade pity, shame

Schaden m damage (n)

Schaf n sheep

Schaffner/in m/f ticket collector

Schal m scarf

Schale f dish

schälen peel

Schallplatte f record (music)

Schalter m switch

Schaltknüppel m gear lever

Schande f shame (n)

scharf sharp, spicy

Schatten m shade

Schaufel f dustpan, shovel, spade

Schaufenster n shop display window

Schaukel f swing

Scheck m cheque

Scheckbuch n cheque book

Scheckkarte f cheque card

Scheibe f slice

Scheibenwischer m windscreen wiper

scheinen shine (vb)

Scheinwerfer m headlight

Schenkel m thigh

Schere f scissors

scherzen joke (vb)

Scheuerbürste f scrubbing brush

Scheuerlappen m floor cloth

Scheune f barn

schieben push

Schiff n boat, ship

Schild n sign (n)

Schinken m ham

Schirm m umbrella

Schlachter m butcher

Schlafanzug m pyjamas

schlafen sleep

GERMAN → ENGLISH

GERMAN → ENGLISH

Schlaflosigkeit f insomnia

Schlafsack m sleeping bag

Schlaftablette f sleeping pill

Schlafwagen m sleeper, sleeping car

Schlaganfall m stroke (medical)

schlagen hit

Schläger m racket

Schlagloch n pothole

Schlagrahm m (used in the south) whipped cream

Schlagsahne f (used in the north) whipped cream

Schlamm m mud

Schlange f snake

Schlauch m hose pipe, inner tube

Schlauchboot n dinghy

schlecht bad, poor (quality)

Schleuder f spin-dryer

schliessen close, shut

Schliessfach n locker

schliesslich eventually

schlimm serious

schlimmer worse

Schlips m tie

Schlitten m sledge, sleigh, toboggan

Schlittschuh m skate (n)

Schlittschuh laufen skate (vb)

Schlittschuhbahn f ice rink

Schlittschuhe mpl ice skates

Schloss n castle, lock (n)

schlucken swallow

Schlüpfer m knickers, panties

Schlüssel m key

Schlüsselbein n collar bone

Schlüsselhalter m key ring

schmecken taste

schmelzen melt

Schmerz m ache, pain

schmerzen hurt (vb)

schmerzhaft painful, sore

Schmerzmittel n painkiller

Schmetterling m butterfly

Schmuck m jewellery

schmutzig dirty

schnarchen snore

Schnee m snow

Schneebrille f snow goggles

schneiden cut (vb)

schnell fast, quickly

Schnellzug m express (train)

Schnitt m cut (n)

Schnittlauch m chives

Schnorchel m
  snorkel (n)
schnorcheln
  snorkel (vb)
Schnuller m dummy
Schnur f string
Schnurrbart m
  moustache
Schnürsenkel m
  shoe lace
Schokolade f chocolate
schon already
schön fine (adj), lovely,
  nice
Schornstein m chimney
Schotte m Scot
Schottin f Scot
schottisch Scottish
Schottland Scotland
Schrank m cupboard
Schraube f screw
Schraubenmutter f nut
  (for bolt)
Schraubenschlüssel m
  spanner
Schraubenzieher m
  screwdriver
schrecklich dreadful
Schrei m shout (n)
schreiben write
Schreiber m pen
Schreibtisch m desk
**Schreibwaren-
  handlung** f stationer's
schreien shout (vb)
Schrittmacher m
  pacemaker
Schublade f drawer

schüchtern shy
Schuh m shoe
Schuld f guilt
Schulden pl debts
schulden owe
Schule f school
Schulter f shoulder
Schürze f apron
Schüssel f bowl
schütteln shake
Schutzhelm m helmet
Schutzimpfung f
  vaccination
schwach weak
Schwager m brother-
  in-law
Schwägerin f sister-
  in-law
Schwamm m sponge
schwanger pregnant
schwarz black
**schwarze Johannis-
  beere** f blackcurrant
Schwarzwald m Black
  Forest
Schwede m Swede
Schweden Sweden
Schwedin f Swede
schwedisch Swedish
Schwein n pig
Schweinefleisch n pork
Schweiss m sweat (n)
Schweiz f Switzerland
Schweizer m Swiss
Schweizerdeutsch
  Swiss-German
Schweizerin f Swiss
schwellen swell

GERMAN → ENGLISH

GERMAN → ENGLISH

Schwellung f lump, swelling
schwer heavy
Schwester f sister
Schwiegereltern pl parents-in-law
Schwiegermutter f mother-in-law
Schwiegersohn m son-in-law
Schwiegertochter f daughter-in-law
Schwiegervater m father-in-law
schwierig difficult
Schwierigkeit f trouble
Schwimmbecken n pool
schwimmen swim
Schwimmflossen f flippers
Schwimmweste f life jacket
schwindelig dizzy
schwitzen sweat (vb)
schwören swear
schwül humid
See m lake
See f sea, ocean
Seekrankheit f seasickness
Seetang m seaweed
Seezunge f sole (fish)
Segeln n sail (n), sailing
segeln sail (vb)
sehen see
Sehenswürdigkeit f sight, place of interest

Sehenswürdigkeiten besichtigen to go sightseeing
Sehne f tendon
sehr very
Sehr erfreut! Very pleased! Pleased to meet you!
seicht shallow
Seide f silk
Seife f soap
Seil n rope
Seilbahn f funicular
sein be
sein/seines his
Seite f page (n), side
Sekretär m secretary
Sekretärin f secretary
Sekunde f second
selbst myself
Selbstbedienung f self-service
selbstversorgend self-catering
Sellerie m celery
selten rare (seldom)
seltsam strange, weird
Semesterferien pl vacation (university)
senden send
Senf m mustard
September m September
Serviette f napkin
Sessel m armchair
Sessellift m chair lift
setzen sit
Sex m sex (intercourse)

Shorts f shorts
sich anmelden
 check in
sich anschnallen
 fasten seatbelt
sich freuen auf look
 forward to
sich kümmern um
 look after
sicher certain, safe
Sicherheitsgurt m
 safety belt, seat belt
Sicherheitsnadel f
 safety pin
Sicherung f fuse
Sicherungskasten m
 fuse box
sie she, they
Sie you (formal)
Sieb n colander, sieve
Signal n signal
Silber n silver
Silvester New Year's
 Eve
sind are
singen sing
Sitz m seat
Ski m ski (n)
Ski fahren ski (vb)
Ski laufen ski (vb)
Skipiste f ski slope
Skistiefel m ski boot
Slowake m Slovak
Slowakei Slovak
 Republic
Slowakin f Slovak
Slowakische Republik
 Slovak Republic

Socken pl socks
Sodawasser n soda
Sodbrennen n
 heartburn
Sofa n couch
sofort immediately,
 straightaway
sogar even
Sohle f sole (of shoe)
Sohn m son
sollte should
Sommer m summer
Sonnabend m Saturday
Sonne f sun
Sonnenaufgang m
 sunrise
Sonnenbrand m
 sunburn
Sonnenbräune f suntan
Sonnenbrille f
 sunglasses
Sonnencreme f suntan
 lotion
Sonnendach n sunroof
Sonnenschein m
 sunshine
Sonnenschirm m
 sunshade
Sonnenschutzcreme f
 sun block
Sonnenstich m
 sunstroke
Sonnenuntergang m
 sunset
sonnig sunny
Sonntag m Sunday
sonst otherwise

GERMAN → ENGLISH

sonst nichts nothing else

Sorte f sort, type

Sosse f gravy, sauce

Souterrain n basement

Souvenir n souvenir

Spanien Spain

Spanier m Spaniard

Spanierin f Spaniard

spanisch Spanish

sparen save

Spass m fun

spät late

Spaten m spade

später later

Spaziergang m walk (n)

Speck m bacon

Speiche f spoke (of wheel)

Speicher m attic

Speisekarte f menu

Speisevergiftung f food poisoning

Speisewagen m buffet car, dining car

Spesen f expenses

Spezialität f speciality

Spiegel m mirror

Spiel n game

spielen play (vb)

Spielplatz m playground

Spielzeug n toy

Spinat m spinach

Spinne f spider

Spirale f coil

Spirituosen f spirits

Spitze f lace

Splitter m splinter

Sporttauchen n scuba diving

Sportwagen m buggy

Sprache f language

Sprachführer m phrase book

Sprachkurs m language course

sprechen speak, talk

springen jump

Sprit m fuel

Spritze f injection, hypodermic needle

sprudelnd fizzy, sparkling

Sprung m jump (n)

Sprungbrett n diving board

Sprungschanze f ski jump

Spülkasten m cistern

Spülmittel n washing-up liquid

Spur f lane (on motorway)

Staatsangehörigkei f nationality

Stachel m sting (n)

Stadion n stadium

Stadt f city, town

Stadtplan m map

Stadtzentrum n city centre

stark strong

Starthilfekabel n jump leads

Station f ward (hospital)

statt dessen instead

Statue f statue
Stau m traffic jam
Staub m dust
Staubsauger m
  vacuum cleaner
Staubtuch n duster,
  dustcloth
Staubwedel m feather
  duster
stechen sting (vb)
Stechmücke f
  mosquito
Steckdose f socket
Stecker m plug
  (electrical)
Stecknadel f pin
stehlen steal
steil steep
Stein m stone
sterben die
Stern m star
Steuer f tax
Stich m stitch (n)
Stiefel m boots
Stiefmutter f step-
  mother
Stiefvater m step-
  father
still still, quiet
Stille f silence
Stimme f voice
Stirn f forehead
Stockwerk n storey
Stoff m cloth, material
Stoppschild n stop
  sign
Stöpsel m plug (bath)
stören disturb

stornieren cancel
Stornierung f
  cancellation
Stossdämpfer m
  shock absorber
stossen knock, push
Stoßstange f bumper,
  fender
Strafzettel m parking
  ticket
Strand m beach
Strasse f road, street
Strassenarbeiten pl
  road works
Strassenbahn f tram
Strassenkarte f map,
  road map, street map
Strauss m bunch (of
  flowers), ostrich
Streichhölzer pl
  matches (for lighting)
Streik m strike
streiten quarrel
stricken knit
Strickjacke f cardigan,
  jersey
Stricknadel f knitting
  needle
Strickwaren pl knit
  wear
Stroh n straw
Strom m electricity,
  current (electric)
Stromausfall m power
  cut
Stromspannung f
  voltage

GERMAN → ENGLISH

GERMAN → ENGLISH

Strömung f current (water)
Strumpf m stocking
Strumpfhosen pl pantyhose, tights
Stück n bit, piece
Student m student
Studenten- ermässigung f student discount
Studentin f student
Stufe f step
Stuhl m chair
stumpf blunt, dull
Stunde f hour
stündlich hourly
Sturm m storm
Sturzhelm m crash helmet
suchen look for, search
Südafrika South Africa
Südafrikaner m South African
Südafrikanerin f South African
südafrikanisch South African (adj)
Süden m south
Summe f amount
Sumpf m marsh
Suppe f soup
Surfbrett n surfboard
süss sweet (adj)
Süssigkeiten pl sweets, candy
Synagoge f synagogue

T
Tablett n tray
Tachometer m speedometer
Tafel Schokolade f slab of chocolate
Tag m day
Tagebuch n diary (personal)
Tageskarte f set menu
täglich daily
Taille f waist
Tal n valley
Tampon m tampon
Tank m tank
Tankanzeige f fuel gauge
Tankstelle f garage, petrol station
Tante f aunt
Tanz m dance (n)
tanzen dance (vb)
Tasche f bag, pocket
Taschendieb m pickpocket
Taschenlampe f flashlight, torch
Taschenrechner m calculator
Taschentuch n handkerchief
Tasse f cup
taub deaf
Tauchanzug m wetsuit
Tauchbrille f diving goggles
tauchen dive
tausend thousand

Taxe f cab, taxi
Taxi n cab, taxi
Taxifahrer m taxi driver
Taxistand m taxi rank
Team n team
Tee m tea
Teebeutel m tea bag
Teekanne f teapot
Teelöffel m teaspoon
Teig m pastry
Teil n part, piece
teilen share (vb)
Telefon n telephone (n)
Telefonbuch n phone book, telephone directory
telefonieren telephone (vb)
Telefonkarte f phone card
Telefonnummer f phone number
Telefonzelle f phone booth
Teller m plate
Tempel m temple
Temperatur f temperature
Tennis tennis
Tennisplatz m tennis court
Tennisschläger m tennis racket
Teppich m carpet, rug
Termin m appointment
Terminal n terminal
Terminkalender m diary (business)

teuer dear, expensive
Theater n theatre
Theke f bar counter
Thermalquelle f hot spring
Thermometer n thermometer
Thermosflasche f flask
Thunfisch m tuna
tief deep
Tier n animal
Tierarzt m veterinarian
Tierärztin f veterinarian
Tinte f ink
tippen type (vb)
Tisch m table
Tischler m carpenter
Tischtennis table tennis
Tischtuch n tablecloth
Tochter f daughter
Tod m death
Toilette f lavatory, toilet
Tollwut f rabies
Tomate f tomato
Tomatensaft m tomato juice
Töpferwaren pl pottery
Tor n gate
tot dead
töten kill
Touristenklasse f economy class
tragen carry, wear
Tragetasche f carrier bag
Tragflächenboot n hydrofoil

GERMAN → ENGLISH

GERMAN → ENGLISH

Trainingsanzug m tracksuit
trampen hitchhike
traurig sad
treffen meet
Treppen fpl stairs
treten kick (vb)
Trinkbecher m mug
trinken drink (vb)
Trinkgeld n tip
Trinkwasser n drinking water
Tritt m kick (n)
trocken dry (adj)
Trockenmilch f powdered milk
trocknen dry (vb)
Trockner m tumble dryer
Tropfen m drop
trübe dull
Truthahn m turkey
Tschechien Czech Republic
Tschechische Republik Czech Republic
Tunnel m tunnel
Tür f door
Türglocke f doorbell
Türke m Turk
Türkei f Turkey
Türkin f Turk
türkis turquoise
türkisch Turkish
Turm m tower
typisch typical

U
U-Bahn f metro, subway, underground
Übelkeit f nausea
üben practise
über over, via
über Nacht overnight
überall everywhere
Überfahrt f crossing
überfallen mugged
überfüllt crowded
Übergewicht n excess luggage, obesity
überhitzen overheat
überholen overtake
Übernachtung mit Frühstück bed & breakfast
überprüfen check
übersetzen translate
Übersetzer/in m/f translator
Übersetzung f translation
Überzieher m overcoat
üblich usually
Ufer n shore
Uhr f clock
Uhrenarmband n watch strap
um at (time)
umdrehen turn around
umgeben surround
Umgehungsstrasse f ring road, bypass
Umkleidekabine f changing room
Umschlag m envelope

umsteigen change (vb)
umstossen knock over
Umtausch m exchange
Umweg m detour
umziehen change
clothes, move house
unbequem uncomfort-
able
unbeschränkt unlimited
**unbeschränkte Fahr-
karte** open ticket
und and
Unfall m accident, crash
Unfallstation f casualty
department
ungarisch Hungarian
Ungarn Hungary
ungefähr about, roughly,
approximately
ungerade odd (number)
ungewöhnlich unusual
unglaublich incredible
ungültig werden expire
ungünstig inconvenient
Universität f university
unmöglich impossible
uns us
unser our
unten bottom (at the),
downstairs
unter among, under
unterbringen put ... up
unterhalb below
Unterhemd n vest
Unterhöschen pl
panties
Unterhose f underpants

Unterkunft f
accommodation
Unterlage f record
(legal)
unterrichten teach
Unterrichtsstunde f
lesson
Unterrock m slip,
petticoat
Unterschied m
difference
unterschreiben
sign (vb)
Unterschrift f signature
Untersuchung f
(medical) examination,
(police) investigation
Untertasse f saucer
Untertitel subtitles
Unterwäsche pl
lingerie, underwear
Urlaub m holidays,
vacation
Urlaubsgebiet n resort

V
Vanille f vanilla
Vanillesosse f custard
Vater m father
Vegetarier/in m/f
vegetarian
Veilchen n violet
Vene f vein
Ventil n valve
Ventilator m fan
verärgert angry
Verband m bandage,
dressing

GERMAN → ENGLISH

Verbandkasten m
first-aid kit
verbessern improve
Verbindung f
connection (elec)
verboten forbidden,
prohibited
Verbrechen n crime
verbrennen burn (vb)
Verbrennung f burn (n)
verderben spoil
verdorben off (food)
vereinbaren arrange,
agree
Vereinbarung f
agreement
Vereinigte Staaten
United States
Vereinigtes Königreich
United Kingdom
vereitert septic
verfault rotten
Vergangenheit f past
Vergaser m carburettor
vergessen forget
vergeuden waste
vergewaltigen
rape (vb)
Vergewaltigung f
rape (n)
Vergrösserung f
enlargement
Vergrösserungsglas n
magnifying glass
verhaften arrest
verheiratet married
verhindern prevent

Verhütungsmittel n
contraceptive
Verkauf m sale
verkaufen sell
Verkäufer m sales-
person, shop assistant
Verkäuferin f sales-
person, shop assistant
Verkehr m traffic
Verkehrsschild n road
sign
Verkehrsunglück n
road accident
verkehrt herum upside
down, back to front
verklemmt jammed
verkocht overdone
verlangen charge
(vb, money)
Verlängerungskabel n
extension lead
verlassen leave (vb)
verlaufen lost
verletzt hurt, injured
Verletzung f injury
verlieren lose
verlobt engaged to be
married
Verlobte/r f/m fiancée
verloren lost
vermieten let, hire out
Vermieter m landlord
Vermieterin f landlady
Vermietung f hire
vernünftig reasonable
verpassen miss (vb,
e.g. bus, train)
verrückt mad

verschieben postpone
verschieden different
verschmutzt polluted
verschütten spill
verschwinden
  disappear
verschwunden missing,
  disappeared
Versicherung f
  insurance
versprechen
  promise (vb)
Versprechen n
  promise (n)
verstauchen sprain (vb)
Verstauchung f
  sprain (n)
verstecken hide
verstehen understand
verstopft blocked,
  constipated
versuchen try
Vertrag m contract
Vertreter m sales rep
Vertreterin f sales rep
Verurteilung f sentence
  (court)
Verwandte f relative,
  relation
Verwandter relative,
  relation
Verwechslung f mix-up
verwirrt confused
verziehen move house
verzögern delay (vb)
Verzögerung f delay (n)
Vetter m cousin (male)

viel lot, many, much,
  plenty
viel Glück! good luck!
vielleicht maybe,
  perhaps
Viertel n quarter
Vierwaldstätter See m
  Lake Lucerne
violett purple
Virus m virus
Visum n visa
Vogel m bird
Volk n folk
voll crowded, full
voll tanken fill up
völlig completely
Vollkornbrot n
  wholemeal bread
Vollpension f full board
vollständig whole
von from, of
vor (vor einer Woche)
  ago (a week ago)
vorbeigehen pass (vb)
Vorderseite f front
Vorhang m curtain
Vorhängeschloss n
  padlock
vorher before
vormittags a.m. (before
  noon)
Vorname m Christian
  name, first name
vornehm posh, fancy
Vorort m suburb
Vorschule f nursery
  school
vorsichtig careful

GERMAN → ENGLISH

Vorspeise f starter
(menu)
vorstellen introduce
Vorstellung f
performance
vorüber over
vorübergehend
temporary
Vorwahl f code, dialling
code
vorziehen prefer
Vulkan m volcano

W
Waage f scales
wach awake
Wache f guard, security
guard
Waffe f gun
Wagen m carriage, car
Wagenheber m jack
wählen choose, dial (vb)
Wählton m dialling tone
wahr true
während during, while
wahrscheinlich
probably
Währung f currency
Wald m forest, wood
Wales Wales
Waliser m Welsh man
Waliserin f Welsh
woman
walisisch Welsh
Walnuss f walnut
Wand f wall
Wange f cheek
wann? when?

waren were
warm warm
Wärmflasche f hot-
water bottle
warten wait
Warteraum m lounge,
waiting room
Warteschlange f
queue (n)
warum? why?
was? what?
Was ist los? What's the
matter? What is wrong?
Was kostet es? How
much is it?
Waschbecken n
washbasin
Wäsche f laundry
Wäscheklammer f
clothes peg
Wäscheleine f
clothes line
waschen wash
Waschen und Legen
shampoo and set
Wäscherei f laundry
Waschlappen m
flannel, face cloth
Waschmittel n
detergent
Waschpulver n soap
powder, washing
powder
Waschsalon m
launderette, laundromat
Wasser n water
wasserdicht
waterproof

Wasserkessel m kettle
Wassermelone f
  watermelon
Wasserski laufen
  water skiing
Watte f cotton wool
Wechselgeld n
  change (n)
Wechselkurs m rate
  (of exchange)
wechseln change (vb,
  money)
Wechselstube f
  bureau de change
Weckruf m wake-up call
weder ... noch
  neither ... nor
weg away
Weg m path, way
wegfahren leave (vb),
  depart
weggehen leave (vb),
  go away
Wegweiser m signpost
weiblich female
weich soft
Weihnachten Christmas
weil because
Wein m wine
Weinberg m vineyard
Weinbrand m brandy
weinen cry
Weinkarte f wine list
Weintrauben f grapes
weiss white
Weisswäsche f linen
weit far, wide
weiter further

weitermachen
  continue
welche/r/s? which?
Welle f wave
Welt f world
wenige few
weniger less
wenn if
wer? who?
werfen throw
Werktag m weekday
Werkzeug n tool
Werkzeugkasten m
  tool kit, toolbox
Wert m value
wert worth
wertvoll valuable
wesentlich essential
Wespe f wasp
wessen? whose?
Weste f waistcoat
Westen m west
wetten bet
Wetter n weather
Wettervorhersage f
  weather forecast
Wettspiel n match
  (game)
Wettspiele pl matches
  (games)
wichtig important
wie how
Wie bitte? Pardon?
Wie geht es Ihnen?
  How are you?
Wie spät ist es?
  What's the time?
wieder again

GERMAN → ENGLISH

GERMAN → ENGLISH

wiederholen repeat
wiegen weigh
Wien Vienna
wieviel/e? how much/many
Wieviel Uhr ist es? What's the time?
Wild n game
Wildleder n suede
Wildschwein n boar
willkommen welcome
Wimperntusche f mascara
Wind m wind
Windel f diaper, nappy
Windeln f diapers, nappies
windig windy
Windpocken f chicken pox
Windschutzscheibe f windscreen
Winter m winter
winzig tiny
wir we
wirklich really
Wirtschaft f economy
wissen know
Witwe f widow
Witwer m widower
Witz m joke (n)
wo? where?
Woche f week
Wochenende n weekend
wöchentlich weekly
Wohnblock m block of flats, apartment block

wohnen live, stay
Wohnheim n hostel
Wohnung f flat (n), apartment
Wohnwagen m caravan
Wohnwagenplatz m caravan site
Wohnzimmer n living room, lounge
Wolf m wolf
Wolke f cloud
Wolle f wool
wollen want
Wort n word
Wörterbuch n dictionary
Wucher m rip-off
wunderschön beautiful
Wunsch m wish (n)
wünschen wish (vb)
Würfel m dice
Wurst f sausage

Z
zäh tough
Zähler m meter
Zahn m tooth
Zahnarzt m dentist
Zahnbürste f toothbrush
Zähne pl teeth
Zahnschmerzen toothache
Zahnseide f dental floss
Zahnstocher m toothpick
Zange f pliers
Zaun m fence

Zeh m toe

Zehe f clove (of garlic)

Zeichnung f drawing

zeigen show (vb)

Zeit f period, time

Zeitkarte f season ticket

Zeitschrift f magazine

Zeitung f newspaper

Zeitungskiosk m news stand

Zelt n tent

zelten camp

Zeltplatz m camp site

Zentimeter m centimetre

Zentralheizung f central heating

Zentralverriegelung f central locking

Zentrum n centre

zerbrechlich breakable

Zeuge m witness

Zeugin f witness

Ziege f goat

Ziegel m brick

ziehen pull

ziemlich fairly, quite

Zigarre f cigar

Zigarette f cigarette

Zimmer n room

Zimmerdecke f ceiling

Zimmermädchen n maid, chambermaid

Zitrone f lemon

Zoll m customs, inch, toll

zollfrei duty-free

Zollstrasse f toll road

Zone f zone

Zoo m zoo

Zopf m plait

zornig angry

zu too (e.g. too much)

zu/zur/zum to

Zucker m sugar

zuckerfrei sugar-free

zuerst at first, first of all

Zug m train

Zuhause n home

zuhause at home

zuhören listen

Zukunft f future

zum Beispiel for example

Zündkerze f spark plug

Zündschlüssel m ignition key

Zündung f ignition

Zunge f tongue

zurückfahren return (in a vehicle)

zurückgeben return, give back

zurückgehen return, go back (on foot)

zurückkommen come back

zusammen together

zusammenbrechen collapse

zusammenheften staple together

Zusammenstoss m crash

zusätzlich extra, additional

zuschauen watch (vb)

GERMAN → ENGLISH

zuschliessen lock (vb)
Zustand m condition
Zutaten f ingredients
zuviel berechnen
  overcharge
zwanglos informal
zwei two, a couple
zwei Einzelbetten
  twin beds
zwei Wochen fortnight
zweimal twice
Zweite m/f/n second
Zweite Klasse
  second class
Zwiebel f onion
Zwillinge twins
Zwischenstation f
  stop-over
Zwischenstecker m
  adapter
Zyklus m cycle
Zyste f cyst

GERMAN → ENGLISH